THE DAWNING OF AN EBONY PRINCESS

An Intriguing Story of God's Deliverance from Multiple Personalities

Celia C. Canterbury

FAMILIES OF VICTORY PUBLISHING

Auxiliary of Families of Victory Ministries, Inc.
The United States of America

FAMILIES OF VICTORY MINISTRIES, INC.
P. O. Box 3075   Lexington, Ohio 44904
celia@fovm.ws   www.fovm.ws

Families of Victory Ministries, Inc. ministers to families who need focused spiritual support and those who are affected by incarceration. We specialize in those who have been abused as well as those struggling in a codependent relationship. Founded, 1989

Library of Congress Control Number: 2005923936

ISBN 1-929385-07-2

Copyright © 2005 by Families of Victory Publishing
First published in the USA by Families of Victory Publishing, Lexington, Ohio

All rights reserved, including the right of reproduction in whole or in part in any form.

Cover design by Aaron Brown, Liberia, West Africa

Nancy L. DeWalt, Editor
Eagle Eye Writing and Editing
P. O. Box 3544
Mansfield, OH 44907
419-756-1011
www.writewing.net

All Scripture quotations, unless otherwise indicated, are from the New International Version of the Bible, copyrighted 1996 by Zondervan Bible Publishers and The Picture Bible copyrighted 1978 by David C. Cook Publishing Company.

Dedication

Without the mercy and patience of my loving heavenly Father, it would have been impossible for me to be victorious in being humble and obedient enough for him to use this precious gift of writing for his glory and honor. Thank You Jesus for selecting me.

To my husband, Nathan

who loves me unconditionally and because of that love remained faithful to our vows to stay together for better or for worse, in sickness and in health.

To my therapist, Eliza

who allowed God to anoint and use her to love me so deeply that she stayed the course until I reached our goal of emotional and spiritual wholeness.

To my mother, Janna Cherie

who introduced me to a saving knowledge of Jesus Christ and encouraged me to write by reminding me that long ago I purposed one day to become an author.

To my editor, Nancy Lorene

who faithfully edited each line challenging me to consider pertinent revisions and keeping hope alive that it would be published.

To every precious soul, Victims of Abuse

that in these pages you will find the hope and courage to become free from all bondages that cripple your walk with the Lord and rob you of peace in your daily relationships.

CONTENTS

DEDICATION ... iii

FOREWORD ... v

PREFACE ... vii

CELIA'S FAMILY OF PERSONALITIES ... viii

CHAPTER 1 ....*It Had to be Perfect*   9
CHAPTER 2 ....*Voices From Within*   19
CHAPTER 3 ....*The Conference Room*   29
CHAPTER 4 ....*The Little Girl Under the Bed*   47
CHAPTER 5 ....*Delivered From The Evil One*   63
CHAPTER 6 ....*The Silhouette of a Princess*   79
CHAPTER 7 ....*Sitting By the Brook With Jesus*   95

APPENDIX A ... 111

NOTES ... 112

BIBLIOGRAPHY ... 114

Foreword

I can still recall the first time I met Celia. She wore a striking red suit and appeared to be so much in command of herself and her world. She was articulate about what she wanted and expected from me as well as thoroughly engaging in her interest in the process of therapy. I could never have known what lay beneath the surface of that seemingly confident exterior on that first day, but our journey together would reveal all the many facets of Celia's life were not as smooth as her first presentation.

Celia is a most intelligent woman. This served her well as she devised coping skills to manage a life shattered by abuse of all types, but it left the emotional realities buried in layers beneath the surface. She was not even aware of these or the extent to which they controlled her life. She was also not aware of the upheaval the unveiling of these layers would create for her or how pivotal her relationship with me would become for a number of years.

Together, we would begin to discover these, and in the process she would become the "ebony princess" that the Lord had intended her to be in the beginning before all the damage and destruction had been done to her heart, mind, body and spirit.

Graduate coursework speaks little of Dissociative Identity Disorder (previously known as Multiple Personality Disorder). Celia presented initially with anxiety and depression. Both are common presenting symptoms for any therapist or counselor, but if we are not keenly aware of what may be going on beneath those symptoms, we will treat the symptoms and miss the core issue. Often that can mean a long history of past abuse prior to and beyond the age of five which resulted in fragmenting the core of the personality. We will overlook the challenge, adventure and joy of discovering God's creative genius in developing a way for us to survive the most heinous abuse. We will also miss discovering His capacity to recreate the core of the personality as He intended in the process of a journey toward healing and wholeness.

The journey began for me when I asked Celia to create a timeline about her life. I could never have anticipated that she would bring me a multi-paged project complete with photographs, drawings, and commentary that would give me my first glimpses into her shattered dreams, shattered hopes and shattered personality. It would serve in the years ahead of us a map for our journey.

No journey we set out on will be without unexpected turns. That was also true of the journey Celia and I were to take. The Lord was a constant companion, but the enemy was a shadow that haunted each step toward healing and wholeness. Sometimes the shadow grew so large and ominous that Celia felt she would not survive. For me, it was a powerful time of always listening for the voice of the Lord to determine Celia's real story and the places the enemy desired us to go that would be a detour from the Lord's purpose and throw us off course and attempt to hinder her move toward wholeness and healing.

The journey taught each of us about ourselves and each other, but above all it taught us more about the Lord Himself.

As you read Celia's story, you may be tempted to consider whether or not it is a true story. Consider carefully before you reject the miracle of the Lord's handiwork. Taste and see that the Lord is good and mighty to the pulling down of strongholds.

I have been forever changed by this journey and I trust the Lord will use what Celia has written to also change you as He desires.

Liz, M.S., LPCC
Marriage & Family Therapist

Preface

God's protection and deliverance from the tragedy of incest empowers a middle-aged woman to live in the present and look forward to the future. The miraculous release from her painful past is recorded here with painstaking detail.

God revealed during an intense therapy session that Celia suffered a devastating trauma at the age of three and a half. Necessity locked the intrusion inside a toddler personality. That creative strategy at such a young age proved extremely effective and became her method of coping with life's challenges.

The Dawning of an Ebony Princess invites you into the private life of an African American multiple who journeyed through caverns of darkness, into experiences of delight -- culminating in the victory of wholeness. Faith in Jesus Christ snatched Celia from the jaws of death and destruction.

If you take this journey, invest in boxes of tissues, experience times of laughter and endure pages of weeping. Yet, at the end of the tears emerges the wonderful story of Celia's victory who dared to take Jesus at his word and trusted her past, present and future to him.

If you have been abused, this book challenges you to pray and to ask Jesus Christ to bring freedom into your life. You can also become victorious. Passing along this "hope" makes this book priceless.

                              Celia C. Canterbury
                              Lexington, Ohio, USA

CELIA'S FAMILY OF PERSONALITIES

Celia created each personality to serve a specific purpose or to escape a perceived trauma. Each one emerged or maintained executive control at will to perform his/her function in the family.

NAME	AGE	DESCRIPTION
Angelica	3.5	An innocent toddler
Celia Kid	5	Kindergartner
Leigha	6	Personification of fear, especially of adults
Tai	8	Asian: an accepted intelligent nationality
Christian	10	A boy who emerges to accept Christ
Celia Sue	11	An angry girl who champions justice
Celia Paul	13	A boy called to preach
Elvira	15	A teen who reacted to her father's death
Wellington	18	A male Austrailian demon (not a personality)
Colleenii Bug	24	A foreign missionary
Gwendolynn	27	A Caucasian created to avoid housing discrimination
C. C.	33	Divorcee
K'Lou	38	African woman created to escape a trauma
Cordella Celia A.	42	The woman who stood at the altar with Nathan
Canterbury	43	The personification of adult hatred
C. Colleenii B. Celia C.	45	The bride who left the church with Nathan
Canterbury	50	A woman emerging emotionally whole and spiritually healthy

CHAPTER 1 ❧ IT HAD TO BE PERFECT

Celia climbed the stairs to her room and crawled under her bed. She felt lower than a snake's belly. She had been misunderstood, betrayed and abused. Any minute her anger would erupt like a volcano. Her parents forbade her to cry, whimper or to express any displeasure whatsoever.

"I'm going to call Children Services. Better yet, I think I'll call the police; I certainly have proof," Celia determined.

An ironing cord had left Celia's arms, legs and back with crimson welts. Her parents' strictest rule was, "If a phone call *beats* you home from school, you will get the *beating* of your life." Although Celia knew the rule, an inexplicable force prevented her from behaving differently.

Underneath her bed became not only her hiding place from the frustrations of life, but the place she comforted herself. Before sliding her hand inside her clothes to massage herself to sleep, Celia recreated the incident that prompted the beating in the first place.

Excitement filled the air. Giggles and shouts sent a chorus of laughter soaring through the trees. Tall and short people, big and little people allowed the breeze to catch their clothes as they swung back and forth, higher and higher. Children, both bold and shy were busy trying to tap a person to become "It," while careful ones and more mature ones talked about swimming, camping and visiting grandparents many miles away.

Designer labels flashed here and there; Buster Browns, Hush Puppies and Saddle Oxfords clothed first-day feet, while Howdy Doody and Mickey Mouse lunch boxes demonstrated that everything was smacking brand new.

The moment finally arrived. A familiar sound burst into their playfulness and commanded respect. Without hesitation, attentions turned to more serious matters. One by one they marched up the steps to greet their new teacher, their new classmates and most of all to enter a new grade.

Standing afar off was an intelligent young girl observing all the activity. She took a step forward as if to join the others, but failed to continue. Her countenance reinforced her hesitation. Once again that piercing sound could not be ignored. She joined the last of the students entering Sojourner School.

Each of us has a story to tell of those good ole school days. Yet for some, those "good ole school days" weren't so good. It is the setting of an old school building that brings intrigue to this story. A strange thing happened in the sanctuary of a sixth grade classroom. Although it had been experienced five times before, this time it did not occur without notice.

What could have happened five times previously without anyone being conscious that it happened? If it had only happened once or

IT HAD TO BE PERFECT 11

even twice, it would be more understandable. Part of this mystery lies within the strokes of the architect's design.

The year was 1913. Neoclassical Architecture became the wave of the future. Robust columns adorned the entrance to each staircase. The large elaborate windows over looked the open stairwell to give a feeling of a larger more challenging world outside. Self-contained classrooms with attached closets and cloakrooms had been individually crafted. Oak desks mounted on black iron scrolled frames bolted to the floor in perfect five rows of seven desks each. "The front row of seats usually didn't have desktops; the students sat there during recitations."[1] Sojourner School beamed with every distinction of neoclassical architecture.

Specialized spaces provided learning enhancement which included a library. "Art and music rooms adjoin the gymnasium and cafeteria and can be joined or separated by a partition wall for maximum flexibility."[2] Finally, an electric bell called every student to a serious day's work.

Kind and gentle described the principal of Sojourner School. Consequently, latecomers were not punished those first three days. One last bell notified several crying children that they were late for school. Needless to say, Celia was not one of them. She knew her classroom, went there immediately and found her nametag at her desk.

Celia beamed with excitement, because this was her last year at Sojourner School. Seventh graders were rewarded with their own school building. She could hardly wait for Junior High, so this had to be her best year ever. With this resolve, Celia set out to do everything perfectly. That's why being tardy was totally unacceptable.

"Good Morning Boys and Girls," Mr. Percival greeted his class for the first time. "This promises to be a special year," he continued. "We have scheduled two major field trips, and those who work hard will be eligible to enter the city-wide Science Fair. New this year is a Young Authors' Conference. I'm certain our class will be well represented," Mr. Percival concluded.

"Wow," thought Celia. "This year will be challenging and lots of fun; I will be the best student in class," she determined.

Celia set out to conqueror her easiest subject first. *Perfect*, that's what her weekly Spelling tablet purposed to show - 100% week after week. The months of September and October rewarded her determination. Not only her weekly tests, but during each Spelling Bee Celia was usually the last one standing.

Unfortunately, one Friday in mid-November, a disappointing phenomenon presented itself, most likely precipitated by the students who dawned the doorway of that particular classroom.

The interior architecture provided for desks lined up in perfectly straight rows. They had to be perfect. Fidgeting chatterers were not tolerated during the course of a tedious school day. So, is it reasonable to expect that they dared presuppose what children might think or do from the time they entered those hallowed walls until the time they departed? If they could imagine a student like Jeremiah Hezekiah Connors walking the halls of that noble building, there is no doubt they would have constructed things much differently.

You are probably wondering, "Who in the world is Jeremiah Hezekiah Connors?" Well, it's impossible to tell this story without including him. His classmates were reasonably convinced that Jeremiah Hezekiah Connors definitely was made of "snips and snails and puppy dog tails." Mischievous didn't even begin to describe him. If there was a student standing in the corner, it was usually Jeremiah. And if a child misbehaved on the playground, that was probably Jeremiah as well. Now he wasn't the only one in class to get in trouble because Celia had her share of staying after school as penance, but the name written on the board most often was Jeremiah Hezekiah Connors.

In this case, however, the spikes took on a life of their own. Logically, inanimate objects are expected to remain where they are placed like desks bolted to a floor.

Not the construction crew, but hundreds of students over the years were responsible for the next chapter that fought its way into Celia's life. One by one and year after year each time a boy or a girl climbed over the rails to take their seats they sowed character into the

IT HAD TO BE PERFECT 13

fabric of the wrought iron construction.

By 1958 more than seventeen hundred students encouraged the spikes to come alive. It was not Jeremiah Hezekiah Connors' fault that years of wear and tear turned his seat into a horizontal rocking chair. Much to his delight Jeremiah had found a way to annoy his classmate.

Jeremiah felt Celia always acted like the best student in the class, so he put together a plan to upset her. He was positive it would work. He put his plan into action on Friday. His timing had to be perfect for it to work.

With a certain pride, Celia looked forward to Friday. Opening exercises passed like a flash. Another school day moved rapidly ahead.

"Will our class monitor please pass out the spelling tablets?" asked Mr. Percival.

Celia opened her tablet and beamed with pride. She counted them 1, 2, 3, 4, 5, 6, 7, 8, 9. Week after week her score was 100% with no mistakes - a perfect record. Not even one word was crossed out and rewritten. Celia appeared to be sailing through her best year ever.

"Make sure your ink bottles are secure in their ink wells," Mr. Percival reminded the class. "If anyone needs a new ink blotter, please raise your hand," his instructions concluded.

"Number 1, a-v-e-r-a-g-e, The average person enjoys sporting events." Mr. Percival did not hesitate to begin their spelling test.

Celia carefully dipped her pen into her ink, blotted the excess and began to write. Suddenly Jeremiah Hezekiah Connors wiggled in his seat causing Celia to miswrite her first word. Her heart began to pound so hard that she allowed a tear to slide down her cheek as she crossed out the mistake and began to write the word again.

Horror bombarded her emotions. *Perfect* no longer described Celia's Spelling tablet. Immediately she thought, "I'll wait before I write my words from now on."

"Number 2, d-e-f-i-n-i-t-i-o-n, A definition tells the meaning of a word." Her teacher continued without noticing Celia's forlorn.

Just as she planned, Celia waited a moment then meticulously wrote the word.

"Number 3, T-e-n-n-e-s-s-e-e, Tennessee was the last Confederate state to leave the Union, and the first to return."

"Number 4."

So far so good, Celia's plan was working. "I can live with one mistake since I know it wasn't my fault," she reckoned.

"Number 19, c-r-i-t-i-c-a-l, Studying hard is critical to a good education."

"And number 20, p-e-r-s-o-n-a-l-i-t-y, Children with a pleasing personality make lasting friends.

"Check your work; leave your tablets open, and pass them to the person in front of you," Mr. Percival instructed.

For the first time since school started, Celia cringed at the thought of passing her Spelling tablet forward. She did not want to give Jeremiah the satisfaction that he had succeeded. Nevertheless, she followed her teacher's instruction and promised herself a viable solution.

Two older brothers, two younger sisters and two younger brothers earned Celia the privilege of being a problem solver when facing new challenges. Domestic responsibilities and seeing after the younger ones defined Celia's lot in life. Daily chores before running off to school included washing a load of clothes, fixing breakfast, washing dishes and combing her sisters' hair. Figuring things out resulted from her mother's silent treatment. So Celia's creativity labeled her a pro at handling difficulties and being resourceful when situations presented themselves.

Seven days marched across the corridors of time more quickly than Celia realized. Friday once again demanded excellence on her weekly Spelling test; she was equal to the task.

"I don't want a repeat of last week's tragedy," thought Celia.

Predictable definitely identified Mr. Percival. "Make sure your ink bottles are secure in their ink wells," Mr. Percival reminded the class. "If anyone needs a new ink blotter, please raise your hand," his instructions concluded.

"Number 1, c-o-m-b-a-t-a-n-t-s, Soldiers become combatants in the face of imminent danger," her teacher began.

Celia made a game out of timing Jeremiah's sway on his horizontal rocking chair.

"All right, one down-- nineteen more to go," she secretly cheered herself to victory.

"Number 2, g-r-a-t-i-f-i-c-a-t-i-o-n, Delayed gratification is its own reward."

The Spelling test continued without incident. Celia's pride filled her emotions.

"Number 17, N-e-w B-r-u-n-s-w-i-c-k, New Brunswick is one of the four Atlantic Provinces of Canada."

Celia once again dipped her pen into her ink, blotted the excess and began to write, but she missed her timing because Jeremiah Hezekiah Connors did something drastically different. He rocked in his seat not once, but twice. The horrible reality forced Celia to write New Brunswick on the next line. Now, she had to cross out her first attempt which made her lines uneven.

Beads of frustration popped out on Celia's forehead. What was she going to do? Number 17 is supposed to be written across from number 7. She could either write number 17 on the very next line or skip a line as expected and write number 17 across from number 8. No matter what she decided, her spelling tablet for the second week in a row screamed, "*Imperfect!*"

"Look, you beaded-eyed pest; stop shaking in your seat during the Spelling test," Celia yelled at Jeremiah during recess. That's all Jeremiah wanted -- the satisfaction that he annoyed Celia.

Even more he was determined to figure out combinations of wiggles and shakes and rocking patterns to force Celia to make a mistake. Of course, calling Jeremiah a 'beaded-eyed pest' guaranteed to saturate him with mischievous behavior.

The anticipated Christmas vacation accommodated Celia's need for a reprieve from her weekly rivalry. Furthermore, she felt a little assistance would be much appreciated.

"Daddy, a boy in my class wiggles in his seat every Friday when I am taking my Spelling test," Celia began.

"He's been making me make mistakes, and he won't stop."

"What did Mr. Percival say when you reported it to him?"

"He said he wasn't going to change my seat, and I shouldn't complain about minor things."

"Celia, don't worry about how your Spelling tablet looks as long as your words are spelled correctly," he replied without taking the matter any more seriously than Mr. Percival.

"Maybe Mama won't think I'm making a fuss over nothing," thought Celia. She was glad she asked her mother and even more pleased she had taken her seriously. Praying about the problem hadn't even entered her mind.

Celia enjoyed her Christmas vacation. She sang in the Junior Choir at Sojourner Community Church. Their Christmas musical promised to be a great success. Butterflies in her stomach meant both nervousness and thrills; it was her first time playing a piano solo as a part of the program.

She wore her new pink satin dress with a petticoat so large it stood out like a minature hula-hoop. An endless spiral of curls rested on her shoulders. Celia's patent leather shoes added to her dashing look as she recited her Christmas poem and played a classical rendition of "O Holy Night."

The message of hope sparked an added support for a solution to Celia's dilemma.

"Lord, please make Jeremiah Hezekiah Connors stop jerking his desk during our Spelling tests," Celia pleaded. Her child-like faith gave her confidence the problem would be settled. She snuggled underneath her blankets and slept peacefully.

Celia believed a new year would bring an inviting and refreshing experience to her Friday tests. After all, she heard it at home; she heard it in Sunday school, and she had read it for herself, "Suffer the little children to come unto me, and forbid them not for of such is the kingdom of heaven." [3]

January 5, 1959 became an unexpected duplicate of September 3, 1958. Excitement filled the air. Giggles and shouts sent a chorus of laughter soaring through the trees. Boys and girls entertained themselves with snowballs flying across the playground. They challenged their ability to avoid being hit.

Once again everything was new. The Christmas season had proven to be quite prosperous. This time, new coats, mittens, boots and hats spoke of wonderful days ahead. When that familiar sound burst into their playfulness and commanded respect, Celia strode two by two up the steps to her classroom. The old year claimed her pensive mood.

Even Mr. Percival made a slight change. Reading, English and Geography became their first subjects of the day. To say Celia was pleased is an understatement. Whenever Jeremiah's swaying caused her to make a mistake, she could rewrite her lesson at home and turn in a perfect paper the following day.

Besides, "Spelling isn't going to be a problem anymore because I prayed," she believed.

Celia took special pride when she wrote the words in her Spelling tablet. She didn't even consider waiting to see if Jeremiah was going to rock in his seat. Unfortunately, the eleventh word threw Celia further into a tizzy than she had ever been. She thought 1958 claimed Jeremiah's mischief, but he continued to be a menace.

Friday after Friday Jeremiah Hezekiah Connors managed to coerce Celia to rewrite at least one word. During several tests, she rewrote two or more words. One week in February her frustration caused her to actually misspell "potato."

A red slash mark and a score of ninety-five percent stared at her. Celia could endure no more. The whole matter saturated her limit. She tried every remedy imaginable, but no relief was in sight.

The clanging of the bell announced that school for the week had come to an end. Row by row the students put on their wraps. In the secrecy of Celia's anger and pain a complex metamorphosis erupted.

"This time I'm going to dismiss the boy's line first," Mr. Percival announced as he cleared his throat.

The boys began to move forward. Celia also began to move forward. That's when it happened for the sixth time. She started to cry and to scream and to hit Jeremiah Hezekiah Connors in the chest, on his head, in the stomach and on every part of his body she could land a punch.

They went tumbling, falling down three flights of sixteen concrete steps each. They rolled head over heels, body upon body, with a thump and a bump again and again. Celia's arms were flailing. Jeremiah's agonizing screams pierced terrified onlookers -- teachers and students alike. The horror continued until their heads smacked into the thick wooden doors on the first floor landing.

CHAPTER 2 ❖ VOICES FROM WITHIN

Liz slowly rolled her chair closer to her client. She gently took Celia's right hand and placed it over her left shoulder. She took Celia's left hand and placed it over her right shoulder and drew her client into her embrace. Celia gasped and sobbed until she sensed Liz saying, "S-h-h-h, s-h-h-h, s-h-h-h everything is all right now; everything is all right."

During the past two years, Celia had awarded Liz with a glimpse that a devastating trauma soiled her life and perspective. And right there before her own eyes Liz witnessed a forty-eight year old woman take on the character, the demeanor and the voice of an eleven-year-old child as she recounted her experience at Sojourner School with Jeremiah Hezekiah Connors.

Liz became concerned why Celia demonstrated such a need to be in control as she held the fragile woman in her arms. Time would not permit any further revelation. Liz waited patiently until Celia composed herself, inquired of her safety to drive home and dismissed her with a prayer.

Eight miles across town presented an adequate distance for an inexplicable stirring to take place.

"My name is Celia Sue; I offer no apologies for showing up the way I did; I just couldn't keep silent any longer. I wanted to tell my own story!" The monologue concluded.

Celia looked around even though she drove alone. She seemed certain she heard a voice.

"That's silly," she reassured herself. Yet there continued to be a nagging at her soul that she indeed heard a voice from within. However, Celia determined not to entertain any further thoughts on the matter.

Celia headed straight for her bedroom crawled under her covers and went sound asleep. Little did she know how often she would frequent her hiding place even though she had already spent a great deal of time there over the past fifteen months.

❖ ❖ ❖ ❖ ❖

Injections of Morphine and Toradol had not taken effect. "Oh-oh-oh," moaned Celia. "My ankle hurts; what happened to me? What happened to me?"

A deep voice responded, "You were hit by a car; you are in the Emergency Room at Mercy Hospital. Try to be still; the medication will take effect in just a few minutes."

Celia tried to put the puzzle pieces together. She struggled to remember even seeing a car. She could only recall standing at the traffic light waiting to cross. Amnesia claimed her ability to become her own witness.

Even with the noisy sirens and health professionals attending other patients, it appeared an eternity before anyone spoke with Celia again.

"Hey Baby, how do you feel? Are you in much pain?" Delighted to hear Nathan's voice, Celia answered slightly above a whisper, "Honey, what happened to me? I can't remember anything after I started across the street. What happened to me?"

Nathan held his wife's hand and began to explain. "A drunk driver in an old van ran the red light and hit you just before you stepped onto the curve. His drunkenness prevented him from realizing he hit you so he dragged you another eighty feet underneath his van."

Celia began to weep. Fear prevented her from sobbing. If she gave herself permission, the tears would refuse to stop.

"I'm here now; try to get some rest. I'm staying overnight. The doctor will operate tomorrow morning," Nathan comforted Celia.

Five hours in surgery encouraged Nathan's adrenaline to overflow. He sat for a moment with Celia's family and a few friends who came to lend their support. Then he decided to nurse a cup of coffee in the cafeteria. Seven hours of waiting brought no news. Nathan continued to pace back and forth.

"The surgery went better than expected," announced Dr. Macon. "I reconstructed her right ankle with nine pins. A seven-inch rod stabilizes her left upper arm. She will be in recovery for several hours," he concluded.

"How long will Celia be in the hospital and what is the extent of her recovery?" Nathan inquired.

Dr. Macon encouraged Nathan and the others to sit down, "She will most likely be on the surgical ward for two or three days then moved to the rehabilitation wing. Hopefully, Celia can be discharged within three to four weeks."

With that the doctor took in a deep breath and continued, "I am uncertain the extent of her recovery. She will need a hospital bed, a wheelchair, a bedside commode and twenty-four hour care for an undetermined length of time."

Patiently, Dr. Macon explained to Nathan and Celia's family

the extent of her injuries.

"We weren't able to repair the torn ligaments in her knee. Three broken ribs produced concerns as well as having injuries on both sides of her body. Keeping Celia under anesthesia much longer than absolutely necessary could have posed unforeseen complications. Most likely post traumatic arthritis will develop in her right ankle and knee," Dr. Macon continued.

"To be honest with you, Mr. Canterbury, your wife is among a rare number of miracle patients. When the paramedics brought her in last night, we didn't think she would live. That's why we scheduled the surgery for today. Therefore, the extent of Celia's recovery depends on her level of determination."

Nathan knew determination could have been Celia's middle name. He also knew his wife would probably return to the classroom. Being an educator captured her pride and joy. January to August promised adequate time for Celia to recover.

Nathan certainly knew his wife. Celia engaged in every possible combination of therapeutic exercises. Discharged after three weeks in rehab encouraged her progress. In April, she abandoned her wheelchair for a walker. And the sunny days of June found her walking independently. Determination became Celia's first, middle and last name.

As hard as she tried Celia failed to commandeer her tears. "I'm so sorry Celia; your ankle will never allow you to walk or negotiate steps adequately enough to maintain the demands of a teaching profession." Dr. Macon said sensitively.

"A disability retirement is my only recommendation. Again, I apologize Mrs. Canterbury, but I am unable to sign a return to work form."

Celia drove home, crawled under her covers and fell asleep.

Painfully, Celia recounted the second devastation that bombarded her life. She thought it was the worse thing that could happen -- forced retirement with a limited income.

❧ ❧ ❧ ❧ ❧

R-i-n-g, R-i-n-g, R-i-n-g, R-i-n-g, R-i-n-g, R-i-n-g. "I have been trying to reach Osmund for two days. I better check on him," thought Celia.

Her pounding brought no results. She slowly unlocked the door and immediately began to fuss.

"Now Osmund knows the doctor told him to stay home until after Christmas. Where could he be?" She scolded.

"I better look around," thought Celia.

Slumped in a praying position on the bathroom floor Osmund gave no response. Hesitantly, Celia walked in and felt for a pulse. Osmund's cold, lifeless body plunged her into denial. Even the paramedic's black body bag labored in vain to mobilize Celia's denial toward reality.

Courageously, she drove to her mother's house to deliver the news. Janna Cherie's second born passed into eternity at the age of forty-nine.

Celia and Osmund shared a special bond. They made plans to champion each other's victories and to worship together more often. This trauma twisted a knife into Celia's heart. More excruciating than anything she overcame earlier that year was losing her brother without any warning of mortality. The setting sun enveloped the western sky, which found Celia once again crawling into bed expecting sleep to rescue her.

The accident in January, the forced retirement in August, and finding Osmund's body in December furnished the impetus for a deep depression. A family outside of anyone's awareness also suffered the same emotional stress that haunted Celia.

The green digital numbers caught Celia's eye.

"Oh my," she thought. "I slept through lunch and dinner."

That represented the least of her concerns. Her strange experience driving home wiggled a path to Celia's consciousness. Needless to say, giving it an audience had to be denied.

The night treated Celia unkindly. She tossed and turned continuously hearing a child's voice say, "My name is Celia Sue; I offer no apologies for showing up the way I did; I just couldn't keep silent any longer; I wanted to tell my own story!"

"My name is Celia Sue; my name is Celia Sue; my name is Celia Sue," eventually faded into silence.

Perplexity and fear crushed all hopes of Celia's attempt to escape the voice. Feeling defeated she allowed her emotions to be swallowed by her experience.

"I have to compose myself; I have always been a problem solver," Celia reassured herself.

Determined to be assertive she walked into her office, found her archive of letters, journals and poems then began to read. A journal page dated 10 September 1994, contained irrefutable evidence.

> "My sessions with Liz have been disturbing.
> Today she identified the scared, angry and hurt
> little girl inside me. I never wanted to admit
> she exists. I don't like the idea of recognizing
> her. I don't like her. I don't like her one bit.
> She cries all the time and is always afraid.
> She's angry too because she doesn't understand
> why life treated her so cruelly."

Celia decided to dialogue with the voice in her head. If she acknowledged her, possibly she would leave and never return.

"Celia Sue, how long have you been silent and why did you insist on telling your story about Jeremiah Hezekiah Conners?"

"I have been silent for thirty-seven years, and the most effective way to announce my existence required telling my story. Your being appalled that I exist denied you the pleasure of knowing me. Besides, I don't cry all the time, and I'm definitely not afraid," spouted Celia Sue.

"That's right; I'm not the only one; our family includes four girls. I'm the oldest. All of us have many things to say to you, and you better listen, too." Relentless and adamant characterized Celia Sue's attitude.

Riddled with confusion identified Celia's plight. She tightened her eyes, put her hands over her ears and shook her head vigorously from side to side.

"Lord, I can't take any more of this. Please make the voice go away. I need help. I don't even know how to pray. Can you hear me, God; can you hear me?"

A torrent of tears and fluids smeared Celia's face, dropped on her clothes and spilled onto her desktop. Even her prayers felt inadequate.

Worship service failed to answer any questions or to bring Celia any measure of explanation and comfort. Sojourner Community Church's reputation for having the most gifted choir proved ineffective in chiseling an "Amen or Praise the Lord" from Celia's lips. Corporate worship could not penetrate her quagmire.

Into her second week Celia confronted an inescapable truth. She began to cry more often. Celia Sue informed her five-year old Celia Kid remained responsible for the crying. Celia felt fearful and began suffering panic attacks. Celia Sue announced that was six-year old Leigha.

"I can speak for myself." A distinctly different voice said hurriedly. "My name is Tai; I'm eight years old. Celia Sue doesn't have to do my talking for me. I am quite capable of representing myself."

Day after day voices bombarded the majority of Celia's waking moments. They would not be quiet. The voices were a bursting dam flowing forcefully and freely with no signs of ever being plugged.

Celia regretted giving Celia Sue an audience. She anticipated one voice, but the idea of four voices thrust her into the depths of despair. She resented being dragged to the brink of reality.

Everyday since her previous session with Liz, Celia repeatedly heard voices. What she thought was the same voice over again manifested themselves as four children invading her adult world. This new realization fitted snuggly into the communicated messages. Celia hated it. Without warning she became reduced to childish voices and embarrassing behaviors.

Celia wanted to erase the past weeks from her calendar. Now she had to reckon with this painful development. Exasperated Celia allowed her frustration to cloud her ability to think. During Celia's smorgasbord of confusion, crying, rocking back and forth, sucking her thumb and carrying stuffed animals, God remained faithful in meeting her needs. Desperate, Celia called Liz. She was relieved to learn Liz was available. They talked extensively.

"Liz, what's happening to me? Do I have a split personality? I've been crying, rocking myself to sleep and sucking my thumb," sobbed Celia.

"Am I going to be all right? Everyday I feel like I am fighting this strange thing inside of me. Am I losing my mind? Liz, please help me; please help me. I don't know what to do. The voices refuse to stop."

Compassionately Liz whispered, "S-h-h-h, s-h-h-h, s-h-h-h everything will be all right; everything will be all right."

"I know you are afraid and have a lot of questions. It would be much better for us to discuss them when we are together. Tell the voices, Liz said, no more talking until Monday."

"As long as you aren't hearing the voices you can handle your daily responsibilities," encouraged Liz. "Only drive when it's absolutely necessary. Extend yourself a little grace and treat yourself to a nice bubble bath," her therapist further advised.

Celia began to calm down just a little, but not enough for Liz's satisfaction. Her client's well-being remained a concern.

"Celia, fix yourself a cup of tea; try to relax over the weekend, and we will establish a Conference Room on Monday to give the girls an opportunity to talk," Liz reassured her.

Pleased with the further calming of Celia's anxiety Liz politely said, "I'm praying for you. Good-bye Celia."

Nathan returned from his business trip early Friday evening. Disappointment captured his heart. Celia usually ran to greet him. He called for her, but received no reply. He bounded down the steps to her office thinking she probably didn't hear him, but no Celia.

Both of her cars were in the garage so he believed she hadn't left the house. Somewhat skeptical, Nathan walked into the bedroom and found her there. To his surprise, an empty teacup sat on the nightstand. Celia was sound asleep with her thumb in her mouth and a teddy bear under her arms.

CHAPTER 3 ❖ THE CONFERENCE ROOM

"A-h-h-h-h-h, A-h-h-h-h-h, A-h-h-h-h-h-h-h-h!" Celia violently shook, screamed and thrashed her head from side to side. A constant cadence of, "A-h-h-h-h-h, A-h-h-h-h-h, A-h-h-h-h-h-h-h-h," pierced the quietness as she rocked back and forth vehemently. Hysterics prevented her from hearing Nathan call out to her.

"Celia, Celia, it's me, Nathan; it's me, Nathan."

"C-e-l-i-a-a-a!" finally penetrated her screams.

Nathan slowly sat down, held Celia tenderly and quieted her terrified heart. Sixty minutes ticked away before her shaking and whimpering completely subsided.

"It's late, Honey, and you've expended a lot of energy. Why don't you retire for the night? Besides, you want to be strong to meet with Liz in the morning. I'll get your medication and stay with you until you fall asleep."

"Lord, I don't know what's troubling Celia," Nathan sighed.

"She's been screaming like that ever since we got married. Tonight really frightened me. She's never reacted that petrified."

"It's been three years, Jesus. I have no idea how to help her. Would you please give Liz wisdom?"

Nathan permitted a tear to slide uninterrupted down his cheek. He knew something horrifying haunted Celia.

⊷ ⊷ ⊷ ⊷ ⊷

Celia had barely been seated when Liz asked, "What's been going on with you, Young Lady? I got a call from Nathan last night. He gave only a sketchy overview, but I need to hear the details."

"I'm not sure I know the details. The television and the carpet muffled Nathan's footsteps. All of a sudden I saw a man standing in the doorway, and I started screaming. It was a man; I didn't recognize him. The next thing I know I drew up in a fetal position sucking my thumb and crying like a baby. I couldn't stop. I don't know why I reacted that way. I just kept crying. I felt like a terrified child. Fear gripped me and wouldn't let me go."

"Have you heard any more voices since Friday?"

"No, the ones I have already heard are more than enough for me. These voices are controlling my life. Whenever I hear a voice, I act like a little kid. I hate it; I hate it."

True to her word Liz discussed the basic rules for a Conference Room. It became the imaginary place where all the personalities met and agreed to take turns being heard.

Rule Number One: Only those in the Conference Room will be given an audience to speak.

Rule Number Two: Each personality must respect the one who is speaking.

Rule Number Three: No one is permitted to interrupt or to take executive control (be the one in charge) without permission.

Rule Number Four: Get to know and accept everyone in the

Conference Room.

"Hi, I'm Tai and I'm eight years old. I'm a Reporter so I should talk first. May I please call you Eliza? Liz is such a grownup name."

"Of course, Tai, you may call me Eliza. How many are in the Conference Room?"

"Celia Kid, Leigha and Celia Sue. I have a secret, and I know what happened to Celia last night."

"I know we just met, Tai, and I can tell you are quite an intelligent little Reporter. Would you trust me with your secret?" Liz gingerly engaged Tai to win her confidence and trust.

"Oh no, I'm not suppose to tell a secret. That's why it's called a secret, but I will tell you this; Celia thought Nathan was Daddy. Daddy used to tiptoe in the bedroom..."

"That's part of the secret, Tai, you weren't suppose to tell that," yelled Celia Sue.

"Rule Number Three: No interrupting, Celia Sue; it's my turn and I'm not finished yet," Tai retorted.

"Girls, girls no arguing. You two are going to have to learn how to get along. Let me speak with Celia," Liz insisted.

Celia looked perplexed when Liz asked her about their conversation. Every word Liz had just exchanged with Tai was completely outside Celia's awareness. She had no recollection of any rules, the argument between Tai and Celia Sue or a secret about Daddy.

"Celia, you have identified four voices and the youngest one is five. Is there anyone younger?" Liz challenged her to consider the possibility.

"I can't imagine how difficult this is for you, but I have to ask, are there any more personalities to be identified?" Liz inquired as she held Celia's hand.

Celia didn't even hear Liz's prayer before she escorted her out of her office. Her concentration captured the audacity Liz wanted her to consider other personalities. That meant more voices and further fragmentation. Wasn't she confused enough? That notion was dismissed before it could even take root.

Celia's resolve was short lived.

A tiny angelic voice announced, "I'm three and a half years old and I have a doggie not a teddy bear. His name is Snuggles, but I don't have a name."

Celia figured it would be wasted energy trying to ignore this newest member of her internal family.

"You sound so sweet and innocent I'm going to name you Angelica," Celia acquiesced.

"Are you the one who is afraid and have been crying and sucking your thumb?"

"I've been crying, but I'm not the only one who sucks her thumb. Celia Kid and Leigha suck their thumbs, too," Angelica defended herself.

Celia's only companion on the way home was silence. Her session with Liz presented more pain than she could face. Thankful Nathan's job carried him out of town, Celia plopped on her bed, revisited her morning and burst into tears.

The weeks turned into months; Tai, Celia Sue, Angelica, Celia Kid and unidentified voices spoke to Celia. Whining, fussing, arguing, tossing and turning during the night and messages so despicable they couldn't be true infiltrated Celia's world.

Desperation affected Celia's ability to think rationally or to make it through a twenty-four hour day without falling asleep in a pool of tears. A common thread existed with each personality -- they loved to write. Necessity forced them to reach out to Liz for help.

Letters flooded Liz's mailbox. Some were mailed, but most were hand delivered. They came written on a variety of stationeries. Many were typed while others were neatly hand written. Tai, the Reporter, claimed executive control regularly. Celia Sue, the champion for justice, took issue with Tai divulging family secrets. Their perplexity prompted this correspondence.

3:30 P.M.

"A Voice in my Head"

Dear Eliza,

I don't know who's talking to me. Oh, she said her name is Cordella. I sure hope you are going to be my therapist at least ten more years. I may need you that long.

So far here is the list:

Angelica	3.5	Celia Paul	13
Celia Kid	5	Elvira	15
Leigha	6	Wellington	18
Tai	8	Cordella	33
Celia Sue	11	Celia Colleen (C. C.)	48

Eliza, I'm not sure how I feel about all of this. Humpty Dumpty comes to mind.

As I am rocking back and forth in my swivel chair I'm not sure of anything anymore. The question that comes to mind, "Are Celia Colleen and C. C. the same?" There is a possibility they are not. Then again perhaps they are. I suppose time will tell.

Some of my mail comes in C. Colleenii B. She's probably another part of me, too. If she is, she's 45 and the one who married Nathan. I'm so fragmented I don't know what difference it makes anyway. To hell with it all! I don't know who wrote that, and I don't much care. Just give me my ticket for the Old Ship of Zion.

Signed,

Whoever I Am

Constant confusion met Celia early in the morning and traveled with her throughout the day. No longer could she deny the ever-increasing voices, but nothing prevented her from refuting the messages. The setting sun found Celia once again groping for sanity. There seemed to be no end to the discovery of personalities. As soon as Celia reckoned with the personalities who previously presented themselves, another strange voice would appear. Week after week Liz concentrated her efforts on identifying how many times Celia had fragmented into new selves. A thorough accounting became critical to Liz's tender care of her client.

Much to her delight Liz received a picture colored by Angelica who remained reticent the majority of the time. However, she made sure she was not forgotten by sending a message she had colored for Liz.

She must have understood not only the meaning of her name, but also the significance of the angel who announced the birth of Jesus. The picture communicated a poignant message that Angelica innocently represented the consequences of being abused. The pure and holy Christ Child was also mistreated even though he did nothing wrong. Neither Jesus Christ nor Angelica became an ultimate victim. Victory etched its mark upon their lives before time began.

Liz depended on the delivering of letters to know if other personalities existed. Each letter became a window into the very depths of Celia's soul. Much to her surprise and delight Liz received a letter from Angelica and someone she would meet in the future. The picture several months earlier had been their only communication. Locked away from any recollection of personal experience emanated horrific stories of unimaginable abuse. Liz was hoping the trauma had not forced Angelica into total silence.

Hi Eliza,

This is Angelica. I wanted to see today. When do I get to talk to Jesus? I got new socks on. I got a new top on to.

C. C. is fat and not littler like me. She lets us eat lots of candy. I love you.

From
Angelica

36 THE DAWNING OF AN EBONY PRINCESS

Howdy there Eliza,

My name is Christian, and I'm a rootin' tootin' cowboy. I'm ten years old. I like Country Western Music; my favorite place to eat is the Ponderosa. Every chance I get I go square dancin', and I just love a fiddle pickin' knee slappin' Hoe Down.

My other favorites are writin', readin' and church goin' I just love myself a good ole sermon to carry me through the week. Mid week prayer service has a way of firin' me right up to do the Lord's will. You might say that the Lord and I are pretty good pals and all.

Now let me tell you about Celia Sue. Although I'm the first boy in the family, that's hard to tell compared to Celia Sue and by the way we act. You see I'm a sensitive kinda fella, and I don't like hurtin' nobody's feelins. I just pray and ask God to take care of my troubles for me.

When I started having problems with Jeremiah Hezekiah Conners, I talked to my daddy and my mama about it and followed their advice. The trouble is the problem didn't stop. I was willing to be patient and let the Lord fight my battles, but ole Celia Sue made her appearance. She had enough of that Jeremiah fella and beat the poor boy all in his head. I felt so sorry for him. Celia Sue has a temper like you wouldn't believe.

Now listen here Eliza, the reason why Celia Sue was confused on Wednesday was because I'm the one who asked Jesus into my heart. That's how I got my name, Christian. I explained to Celia Sue all about how I was different and all and I wasn't prone to violence. I told

her that the Lord would have taken care of the problem if she had just been willin' to wait on him.

I know I don't sound like the rest of my family, but I know the Lord has had his hands on me ever sine I can remember. Celia Sue took charge and I've been silent ever since. One of these days right soon I'm comin' to meet ya. Until then,

> See ya later partner,
>
> C. Christian Abernathy

A few weeks after Liz received this letter, Christian kept his promise. He dressed up in a cowboy getup and visited Eliza. Their meeting was a bit tearful, but definitely delightful.

"Well howdy there Partner; I don't have to tell you that I'm Christian. How'd you like my new cowboy outfit? I told Celia it's about time for me to meet ya, and I sure wasn't gonna come dressed like a girl."

"Hello Christian, it is my pleasure to meet you. Your outfit is quite dashing. Ever since I received your letter, I have been looking forward to meeting you."

Liz had a way of greeting, respecting and making Celia feel at ease in her presence. She encouraged all the personalities to express themselves in whatever vernacular was appropriate.

"Tell me, Christian, what would you like to talk about today?"

"I've been in the Conference Room listenin' and decided it was time fa me to make a personal appearance. Tai and Celia Sue especially are always talkin' about how much they love ya and all. I guess the truth of the matter is I just got a little bit jealous, Ma'am. I figured I had to come so I wouldn't feel left out of the conversations."

"I'm glad you came. I know feeling left out is uncomfortable. It pleases me to know that you have been in the Conference Room and listening to your sisters."

Liz chose her words carefully, "Christian, is there another reason why you came today?"

Christian's eyes became wide as saucers. He stared at Liz, but didn't say anything for a moment or two. Tears began to flow freely. Christian opened his mouth, but his voice failed him.

As Liz had done on so many ocassions with each personality she rolled her chair close to Christian and drew him into her embrace. No words were necessary. Liz recognized his painful countenance. She had seen it innumerable times in the eyes of his sisters.

Celia's fragmentation into different selves required extensive therapy. Each personality needed his/her own audience with Liz. Meeting once a week quickly became inadequate. Twice a week was also short lived. Monday, Wednesday and Friday at 8:00 A.M. became the hour of great anticipation for both Celia and Liz.

A cup of orange juice in her family room accompanied Liz each morning during her Quiet Time. She communed with God and listening intently for his direction and guidance for imparting his truth and perspective into Celia's heart. Each session was a new adventure because Liz had no idea who would present in her office and how to meet their needs without God's wisdom.

One Wednesday in June, Liz was greeted by a client wearing this mask. It was 8:00 A.M. so she at least knew it was Celia. Confident a forty-eight year old woman wouldn't wear such a mask she knew it was one of the personalities into which Celia had become to face a trauma in her life. Was the mask a representation of something horrible in Celia's past? Liz whispered a quick prayer, "Lord, fill me with your Holy Spirit and give me a double portion of wisdom for this hour."

"Good Morning, Eliza, guess who I am?" Without allowing Liz to answer, she continued. "I'm Celia Sue; can you guess why I'm wearing this mask?"

"No, Celia Sue, but I would be happy to hear the reason from you. You are so creative; I can't imagine why you might be wearing that mask."

Liz always validated Celia and responded with words pregnant with God's love.

Celia Sue snatched the mask from her head and beamed with expectation.

"How do you like my new hair style? Celia took all of us to the beauty parlor yesterday and gave us a perm. I didn't want you to see it in the waiting room. I wanted to surprsie you in your office."

Liz was pleased and relieved that the mask carried no deep significant message and that she was able to say, "Celia Sue, your hair is quite becoming. I like it very much."

There were times when Celia came with elaborate hair styles that were quite unbecoming. It was not only Liz's calling to help Celia overcome the trauma in her past, but to provide godly encouragement so Celia would embrace every aspect of her own feminity.

An endless parade of wigs, hair pieces and boyish bobs presented in Liz's office. From toddler clothes with ribbons and barrets in her hair to suits and ties with a masculine flair challenged Liz's resolve for ongoing therapy. God trusted Liz with the awesome responsibility of demonstrating the love of Jesus Christ. Her focus demanded maintaining God's purpose for Celia's life.

The Conference Room continued to fill up with more and more personalities identifying themselves as Celia's family. Not long after Liz had the wonderful opportunity of meeting Christian, she received this letter from someone she didn't know existed.

Dear Eliza,

This is a letter written from the depths of my emotions. Would you please tell Nathan that I am not his wife. He has to take care of himself. I am not willing to take care of him. If he really loved Celia, he would take care of her rather than asking her to take care of him. He lets her drive. Nathan must be in denial. He refuses to admit Celia has a problem.

Really Eliza, Celia isn't the one who is actually driving. I have been driving these past several days as well as Elvira before me. I wish there was some way to make him understand that he needs to be a man who can think about how to take care of his wife. The only thing Nathan knows is to work and to bring his money home.

Any glimpse of normalcy is interpreted as total wholeness for Celia as far as Nathan is concerned. I HATE THAT MAN! Celia would do better without him. I also hate it when Celia is affectionate with him. I think he is stupid; I hate stupid people who don't have a brain in their heads. Nathan has a computer chip with very little memory.

I have never written to you, but I am Colleenii Bug. I refuse to tolerate ignorance. Nathan is an ignorant man. He doesn't think for himself. He expects life to be routine. If anything arises that requires a change of action, he is totally lost.

I especially hate it when Celia is thoughtful and kind to Nathan. What really makes me want to puke is when they make love. Celia acts like Nathan is a Prince in Shining Armour.

Oh well, enough about Nathan, I don't talk much, but I sure can write. I apologize that we did not have the privilege of meeting under different circumstances.

This is the very single,

Colleenii Bug

God's faithfulness in Celia's life manifested itself in so many ways. First of all, he gave Celia a wonderful husband whose patience and kindness carried them through the valley of an extremely trying period in their marriage. When Nathan came home from work, he never knew who would greet him. Sometimes Celia was a responsible adult, but most often she was a child demonstrating child-like behaviors. Nathan's Christian character and integrity provided the stability needed to weather

THE CONFERENCE ROOM 41

the stormy days, weeks, months and years of Celia's emotional instability.

Another provision God made was providing Liz's husband, Ray, who was also a Christian therapist, to meet with Nathan twice a month. Once a month the four of them met in a group session to help Nathan and Celia to survive the trauma that invaded their lives.

Letters, Celia's individual therapy sessions three times a week, Nathan's bi-monthly sessions, joint marriage counseling once a month, inumerable phone calls, E-mail and cards delivered by the postal service comprised the majority of God's therapy strategy. Liz never knew what kind of stationery would greet her whenever she opened a letter. Different stationery indicated a new personality was communicating with her and would then join the Conference Room.

Dear Liz,

You told Celia the Monday before she went to Jamaica that you were going to give her some information. When I decided to write to you, I thought I would use your strategy and first give you some information. I'm Elvira. I thought it was about time for me to write to you myself. Celia is so confused right now she is getting a lot of things mixed up.

I like you. You are taking very good care of dear ole Celia. She needs a lot of help right now. She has needed this help for a long long time. She still doesn't realize how much you love her even though you have demonstrated it over and over again. It is going to take a while for Angelica and Celia Kid to grow up, for Leigha to stop being afraid and for Tai to stop comforting all of us because Celia is still having problems with this whole phenomenon called love.

Let me tell you something about myself. I'm fifteen years old. Without Celia ever truly understanding how much God loves her and how he has taken care of her, I have had the privilege of knowing God for myself. God has intervened in my life and healed me.

Liz, there is another part of Celia. His name is Celia Paul; he's thirteen years old. He's the preacher. It was Celia Paul who fought and struggled with me about my sinful behaviors.

One of these days I will come out of the Conference Room and meet you face to face. You're quite the therapist, and we appreciate all the prayers and hard work you are doing on our behalf.

> Lovingly,
>
> Elvira

Several letters came unsigned; others were signed, Me. Liz received quite a few letters with the signature, Whoever I Am.

Dear Eliza,

It's four o'clock in the morning; I can't sleep, and I don't know who I am. Maybe I'm Tai because I was the messenger for the gift. Maybe I'm Celia because I made the decision. Maybe I'm Angelica or Celia Kid because we love surprises. Maybe I'm C. Colleenii B. because I was the chauffeur, and I knew the contents of the envelope. Whoever I am and for whatever reason, I do know what I am; I am disappointed, plain and simple. Why haven't I heard from you?

> With love to Eliza,
>
> From Whoever I Am

Experiencing disappointments often resulted from selves being unaware of the communication of the others or Liz's response. Daily encounters remained outside of each one's awareness. So the next week Liz received this letter on unfamiliar stationery.

Dear Liz,

It was I who answered the telephone yesterday. C. C. was rude to me when you called her name. She pushed me aside and said, "How did you know that was me?" We sound alike so it's not possible to tell us apart on the telephone. I'm the shameful 42 year old Cordella. You don't know me, but I could have introduced myself then let you talk with C. C. When she's excited or in pain, she forgets her manners. That's no excuse for her behavior though.

Liz, I wish I had a friend, a real friend. I wish I had a girlfriend that I enjoyed being with -- someone with whom I could share what I'm going through who would walk with me day by day. I'm in pain because I feel lost in a world that holds so much promise for me. The difficulty is the promise seems to be just beyond my reach. I wonder how much longer I am willing to fight to be free to be all God purposes me to be. I am the most wicked of all the sisters. One day maybe I will tell you why.

Liz, I sure would appreciate it if you would be kind enough to schedule an appointment *just for me* so we can talk about my struggles and to give me a hug.

With sincerity,

C. Cordella Canterbury

The parade of stationery stopped with Cordella's correspondence, but the letters continued. Each time Liz met with Celia she received at least one letter. There were many times when she took time to read two or even three letters at the beginning of their session.

One Monday morning Liz was caught quite by surprise.

"Good Morning Liz, I thought it was about time for me to meet you. My name is Gwendolynn; I'm 27 years old. I decided to be my own letter in person."

"Well Gwendolynn, it is my pleasure to make your acquaintance. How long have you been in the Conference Room?"

"I haven't been in anybody's Conference Room. What's that anyway?"

"The Conference Room is the place where Celia's family meets and takes turns talking with each other and with me during our sessions."

"Oh, I thought that was a boxing ring. Everyone has been fighting and calling each other names because of the stories they have been telling each other. I thought you needed to know; that's why I came today."

"Do you know what they are fighting about?"

"Yes, but I think each one should tell you his/her own story. Twenty voices makes for quite a battlefield. There is also someone there named Penelope who is the instigater. She keeps stirring up trouble. She really doesn't seem to be a part of our family. There's something terribly wrong with her. If she weren't there, we probably would get along much better."

Liz tucked that bit of information away for further investigation.

"Celia, I need to have you present. Please come out of the Conference Room."

"Hi, Eliza, I wanted to come in the first place, but Gwendolynn insisted. Since she had never met you, I gave in to her. Were you surprised that she's white?"

"No I wasn't, Celia. You are such a creative and gifted woman that I received Gwendolynn as a precious part of who you are. After all Tai is Asian, Christian is a cowboy, Wellington is Australian and K'Lou is African. It is a privilege for us to be working together; you enrich my life."

That is one of the things that Celia loved about Liz. She accepted her just the way she was and never doubted her sincerity and willingness to become what God created her to be.

"Celia, would you please tell me what's going on in the Conference Room?"

"Celia Sue has been crying and fussing because Angelica, Celia Kid and Tai have been telling stories about Daddy. They are bad stories; I mean real bad stories. Celia Sue doesn't want to believe them."

A stoic expression etched its way onto Celia's face. Fear paralyzed her. She thought Liz was going to ask her to repeat the stories.

Instead Liz cleared her throat and announced, "I want everyone in the Conference Room to stop talking to each other. No more telling stories. I will be the one listening to everyone's story from now on. All of you are going to have to get along. You are a family; you need each other."

Liz bowed her head and prayed for Celia to get some rest from the voices and confusion that infiltrated her life.

"Celia, when you come on Wednesday, we will get to the bottom of all this fussing and fighting."

CHAPTER 4 ❖ THE LITTLE GIRL UNDER THE BED

"Eliza, Eliza, Eliza, the girls aren't doing what you said. You said no more sharing information. First it was Angelica, then Celia Kid, then Tai. Leigha is the only one who is being a good girl and doing what you said. She said Daddy put doggie do-do on her thumb because she wouldn't stop sucking it, and she's afraid not to do what grown up people tell her to do. Leigha said she doesn't want anything bad to happen to her so she's not talking."

Celia Sue was glad Leigha wasn't talking, but she was mighty furious with Angelica, Celia Kid and Tai. She had no intentions of listening to anything that was totally false. There was no way she would allow her ears to be a party to such lies about Daddy.

"Angelica, Celia Kid and Tai said they are mad at me because I don't want to tell you anything. Eliza, that's not true. I don't remember any of those things happening. Lies, lies, and more lies. I don't care if I get in trouble for saying the girls are telling lies on Daddy. What they said is much more than just telling a story. They are trying to ruin Daddy's memory, and I'm not going to let them. Daddy loved us and treated us special."

"I don't care if you believe me or not, Celia Sue, but Daddy rubbed between my legs," Angelica screamed to get her point across. She definitely wasn't going to let Celia Sue bully her just because she was three years old. She maintained enough spunk to defend herself.

"It is true, Celia Sue, because Daddy rubbed between my legs lots and lots of times. That's how I know he loved me. He made me feel good. He told me that all the time."

"Daddy, wouldn't do such a thing. Why are you telling stories about Daddy?" Celia Sue determined not to place any credibility in Angelica's words no matter how spunky she communicated what she believed.

Celia Sue pressed on. "Eliza, I thought Celia Paul and I were best pals, but now he is taking the other girls' side. He said he's not taking sides; he just asked me a question. 'Why was I protecting everybody, and how did Tai learn to comfort us?' I don't know, Eliza. I just know that I'm not going to protect them anymore. I'm going to protect Daddy and Osmund. They didn't say anything about Osmund this time, but they might try to say more mean things about him, too. Eliza, please tell the girls to be quiet. I'll make sure everyone is present and accounted for when you talk to us."

Celia Kid interrupted: "I want Eliza to know that's the same thing Daddy told me. He sucked between my legs all the time. Then he would say, 'I make you feel good; that's how you know I love you.' So you don't have to believe Angelica or me, but it happened just like I said it did. Playing Hospital was Daddy's favorite game."

Celia Sue was beside herself with anger. She refused to believe the words that adamantly pierced her ears. She knew Daddy loved her too, but to entertain the thought that he only loved her for sexual favors was more than Celia Sue was willing or able to consider. Just when she thought she had heard enough, Tai joined the chorus of information.

"Daddy promised me a new piano if I would keep our secret. Daddy played between my legs with pencils and sticks and things. I never told our secret to anyone," Tai added with remorse. "I was always a good patient for him, but I never got my new piano. I'm mad at Daddy; he never kept his promise. I'm glad he's dead."

Liz expected the Conference Room to be spirited by Wednesday, but the barrage of information needed a special anointing of God's grace in order to address their painful recollections. She quickly bowed her head and whispered a prayer for wisdom and guidance.

"Girls, girls calm down. I can only listen to one of you at a time. First of all, I believe all of you. Celia Sue, why don't you meet with me first? Angelica, Celia Kid and Tai, I want you to rest your heads on the table and relax. There will be no more sharing information, do you understand?"

"Yes Eliza, we understand, but when will we get to tell our story?" asked Angelica.

"I'm not sure how much time we'll have. I will try to talk with you and Celia Sue today. Then I will talk with Tai and Celia Kid on Friday. How will that be?" Liz spoke gingerly to further calm their anxiety.

Of course it was Tai, the Reporter, who responded. "That will be all right as long as we can get a hug before we leave today."

"That sounds like a plan. Each of you can have a hug at the end of the session."

With a tear in her eye, Liz turned her attention to Celia Sue. "Tell me, Young Lady, do you have a story about Daddy you would like to tell me? I need to understand why you don't believe your sisters."

"I don't want to remember my story about Daddy. I just know when they tell their stories, I feel bad and want to cry. I'm a big girl; big girls don't cry."

"Celia Sue, it's all right to cry. Everyone cries for different reasons. I cry when anyone special to me passes away. Some people cry even when they're happy. There's nothing wrong with letting your heart cry."

"I can't let anybody see me cry. I was never allowed to cry; so I go upstairs and crawl underneath my bed and cry by myself."

"Why do you crawl under your bed?"

"Because I'm a bad, bad girl, and that's the only place in my house where I belong. I feel safe there."

"What makes you afraid?"

"I'm afraid Daddy will be mad at me because I don't want to play a game with him. He might try to find me so we can play Martin Wilbur, M. D. I have to come into his office (the bathroom) and pretend I need a shot. He said the water needs to run so no one will disturb us. The shot goes between my legs. It's wet and smells bad. I hate to play that game, but Daddy said it's his favorite game. That's how I know Angelica and Celia Kid are telling a story. Hospital can't possibly be his favorite game; Daddy wouldn't lie to me."

Despite her efforts Celia Sue lost the struggle. Tears began to stream down her face. Liz rolled her chair toward her client and compassionately pressed Celia Sue's head against her chest.

"S-h-h-h, s-h-h-h, s-h-h-h, It wasn't your fault. I need for you to hear me. It wasn't your fault. You are not a bad girl, and you're safe now. Daddy can't hurt you any more."

Secretly Celia Sue was glad she could no longer hold back the tears. She found strength and comfort in Liz's arms. No one had ever held her so tenderly. She felt protected and safe.

"Are you going to be all right until the next time we meet?" Liz inquired before giving Celia Sue permission to return to the Conference Room.

"Yes, I'll put my head down and go to sleep. I feel really tired."

Before Liz could respond, a tiny voice greeted her.

"Hello Eliza, I could hardly wait until you were finished with Celia Sue because I wanted my turn today like you promised. I thought she was going to take up all the time."

"It's nice to see you Miss Angelica."

Overwhelmed by the reality of it all Angelica stuck her thumb in her mouth and began to twist her hair into little knots. She rocked back and forth and looked all around.

"Welcome to my office. I'm so glad you came today. I want to hear your story about Daddy, but you're going to have to take your thumb out of your mouth so we can talk. Do you think you can do that?"

The soft lights and Liz's motherly voice encouraged Angelica to slide her thumb out of her mouth and into her lap. Surprisingly, she also stopped rocking.

"I don't know any more about Daddy," she began. "We played *ring around the rosy a pocket full of posies, ashes, ashes we all fall down.* When Daddy fell down, he always got hurt. He thought I got hurt, too because he would rub between my legs to make me feel better, then I had to rub between his legs to make him feel better. I didn't tell Daddy, but I never ever got hurt. Daddy got hurt every time. I wonder why he always wanted to play that game if he got hurt all the time? Maybe because he felt better after I rubbed him."

"Eliza, I don't want to talk any more about Daddy. I wanted to see you so I could get a hug and ask you to please be my mommy. I need a mommy real bad. Tai always says, 'Eliza is my mom; Eliza is my mom.' And I want a Mommy, too."

Angelica began to cry, suck her thumb and squeeze Snuggles who had been sitting in the chair beside her.

Liz held Angelica tightly and sang softly in her ear, "Jesus loves you this I know for the Bible tells you so. Little ones to him belong; they are weak, but he is strong. Yes, Jesus loves you, yes Jesus loves you. Yes, Jesus loves you for the Bible tells you so."

Then she whispered, "For as long as you need me I will be your mommy."

Angelica fell asleep craddled in Liz's arms safe, peaceful, calm and content.

❦ ❦ ❦ ❦ ❦

For the remaining hours of Wednesday and all day Thursday there was trouble in the family. Angelica for the first time was permitted to tell her story and bragged that Eliza believed her. Celia Sue fumed at the recollection of her conversation with Liz. Frustration overwhelmed her with no recourse except to verbally attack anyone in her path.

"Be quiet, Angelica; Eliza said for us not to be sharing information. If you don't stop, I'm going to hurt you."

"You don't scare me; besides, I'm not giving information--so there."

Tai came to Angelica's defense. "Celia Sue, I'm telling Eliza you said you were going to hurt Angelica. She said we have to be nice to each other. You are being mean, real mean."

"I don't care what you tell Eliza you ole tattletale. You're always reporting to Eliza. Go ahead and tell her. You need to mind your own business. And Eliza is going to take my side about that."

Tai stomped up the steps, crawled under the bed and comforted herself to sleep.

The bickering continued for two whole days. Celia, glad it was finally time to go to bed, turned out the lights and slipped under the covers hoping she could get some sleep.

Exhausted, she dragged herself out of bed. The girls kept her up most of the night. Their voices were constant, angry and vindictive. Anxieties and emotions were totally out of control. As silent as they had been in the past they were equally abusive now. At least it was Friday, so Celia hoped Liz could bring some relief to her upheaval.

"Eliza, I comforted us two times and two other times Celia Sue stopped me. Celia Sue is mean to me. She called me a tattletale. She said you are going to take her side today. I told her that Eliza doesn't take sides. Celia Sue is being bad. She said she's going to hurt Angelica if she didn't stop bragging that you believed her. I told her you said we are suppose to get along. Celia Sue said she didn't care. That's when I told her I was going to tell on her then she called me a tattletale. She's just mad because you told her to stop pouting when you called us yesterday. I wish Celia Sue didn't have to come with us."

"Tai, let's start with a hug today. I want you to calm down. Celia Sue is hurting; we talked about some very painful things on Wednesday. You must forgive her and be nice to her anyway. She will be all right. Will you please do that for me?"

"Yes, Eliza, I always want to do my very best for you. You're my mom, and I love you."

Liz perceived she was no longer talking with Tai. Celia's shy expression and the lack of tremendous anxiety told her another personality had automatically taken executive control.

"My, my who have we here? I know you're not Tai; please tell me your name and how old you are. And who is that you have with you?"

"I'm Leigha, and I'm six years old, and this is Pooh."

"I have a special chair for Pooh; let him sit beside you so we can talk."

"Oh no, I have to have Pooh to protect me."

"Celia Sue told me you are afraid of grown-ups. Leigha, I love you; I will never hurt you. I promise to be kind and gentle, but you can still hold Pooh for as long as you want."

"I raised my hand at school because I had to go to the bathroom, but my teacher wouldn't let me. She let the other boys and girls go when they raised their hands. I tried to hold it, but I couldn't. I peed on the floor. My teacher was mad at me, and I got a whipping because Mama had to come to school to bring me more clothes. Grownups are not nice to me."

"I'm so sorry that happened to you. I sure am proud of you for being brave. Thank you for coming and trusting me."

"I came to get a hug and to ask you to be my mommy who won't beat me."

Liz wrapped her arms around Leigha and promised never to beat her. Much to her delight Leigha's whole body slowly relaxed, and dear ole Pooh dropped to the floor.

Liz glanced at the digital numbers. God's timing was always perfect. There was no immediate need to arouse Leigha from her quiet slumber. She, too, relaxed from their intense session then invited God's comfort and protection to accompany Celia home.

So many amazing components made this journey with Celia fascinating. As the personalities occupied the Conference Room they began to respect each other's need to talk. Those who needed an audience before they had an opportunity to meet with Liz would write. Liz looked forward to the letters because they provided added insight.

Hi Eliza,

C. Colleenii B. said, "You girls can do better." So I made the bed today. Not real good, but kinda good for an eight year old. Celia Sue is mad at you, and she didn't help us clean up either. Celia Paul hung up our clothes on the bed, and Elvira put up the clothes from our trip to Arizona.

Celia Sue is pouting. She's mad because you talked to Leigha yesterday and you believe what Leigha said. And I'm mad at Celia Sue because she's mad at you. She shouldn't be mad at you. Celia Sue doesn't want to believe anything ever happened to us. She should be glad that Leigha was smiling yesterday. Leigha said, 'Tell Eliza I love you.'

Celia Sue is mad because Celia said she is like her daddy. She doesn't want to believe that Daddy did anything bad because she loves Daddy and always enjoys being just like him. Celia Sue knows the things that Elvira and her brother did together, the things Colleenii Bug and her roommate did together and the things that Cordella and ABC did together. I know because Celia Sue told me. If she's like her daddy, then maybe Daddy did the things we told her he did and that makes her a real bad girl. Celia Sue is also mad at Celia Paul for asking her those questions. And I don't care if she calls me a tattletale either. I thought you needed to know.

I love you, Eliza. Thanks for being my mom. I'm glad you believe Leigha. I hope you believe me too. My secrets are really bad. Oh, I will try to be nice to Celia Sue even if she is mean to me.

Love, Tai

Liz tucked the letter away in her heart. She knew there would be an enormous road to travel. Celia had fragmented herself into so many selves. Receiving the letters made her responsibilities a little more manageable.

Hi Eliza,
    This is Tai. Celia Sue is mad at you so she packed her bags and left and nobody has heard from her since. I don't know where she is. She didn't tell me because she knows I would tell you so you could find her.
    Eliza, Celia Sue doesn't know you love her bunches and bunches and bunches. I know because I heard you. Thank you for calling us from home; that's special. We're special to you, huh Eliza? I'm sorry we make you cry, but I'm glad that crying is okay even when I grow up crying is okay, huh Eliza?
    I'm sorry I was a bad girl again. I tried not to be a bad girl. If I promise never to comfort us again, do you think Celia Sue would come back home? I know she's mean to me sometimes and calls me a tattletale, but Celia Sue is my sister, and I love her. I don't want her to be gone. I just want her to let me be in charge and stay here. If she would come back, I don't even have to be in charge. I don't even know how to reach her so I can tell her.
    Bye Eliza, I just wanted to tell you about Celia Sue.

Love, Tai

Liz remembered reading, "Most alters have only a certain level of negative feelings they can tolerate, and when that level is reached they disappear."[1] Consequently, she was not alarmed when she read Tai's letter even though she thought leaving was a bit extreme.

R-i-n-g, r-i-n-g, r-i-n-g, "Hello."

"Hello Tai, I received your letter today. Are you and the girls all right? How are Christian and Celia Paul? I know having Celia Sue gone is a bit upsetting."

"How did you know it was me?"

"I know your voice, and since you are a Reporter, you have been the one I have been talking with lately. You like to "scoop" a good story about how everyone in the family is getting along. You also have a very cheery voice."

"Celia Paul said he's going to find Celia Sue and bring her back when she gets ready. He said she doesn't need to be by herself. What will I do with both of them gone?"

"I will send you a surprise in the mail. It will be something special you can keep. I know you like surprises. Who knows, maybe Celia Sue will decide to come back by the time you get it? May I please talk with Celia?"

"Hello Liz, thank you for asking to speak to me. I'm really struggling. There are times when I seem fine and I function like an adult then in the next instant I'm Tai, high strung and anxious. With Celia Sue and Celia Paul gone, I feel like a part of me is missing. I just don't know what to do. Will I ever be all right?"

"I called to assure you that you are going to be all right. When a part of you is overwhelmed, s/he might disappear. That's only for a season. Celia Sue keeps fighting her story. When she's ready to accept the truth, she'll be back. Try to relax and permit Tai to be herself. She will eventually calm down. I'll see you Monday."

The bright sunshine lifted Celia's spirit as she drove across town for her appointment. It seemed as though Monday morning would never arrive. The weekend's challenge kept her exhausted and spending more time tossing and turning than she welcomed.

"Good Morning, Tai. I see you're wearing your favorite color today."

"I wore lavender so I can be brave and tell you my story. More than anything else in the whole wide world I want to be a good girl. I don't want to be a bad girl anymore. If I am a good girl, maybe Celia Sue will come back because she hates it when I am a bad girl.

A lot of things have been bothering me. Ever since C. Colleenii B. married Nathan, I've been getting scared. I have been screaming and screaming and screaming. Nathan would say, 'Celia, it's me.' It wasn't Celia screaming; it was me, Tai. Then I would cry and cry and cry. It takes a long time for me to calm down -- sometimes hours.

Celia Sue told me that Andy wasn't the first boy to pull my panties down. Osmund was, and that's why I loved him more than the rest of my family. When we were in Vermont, Celia Sue said Osmund taught me how to comfort myself. I don't know who taught me. I just know that it makes me feel good and bad at the same time. I know it is something I shouldn't be doing because I would do it in the bathroom or under my bed."

By this time Tai is rocking in her chair and twisting her hair into little knots and bawling. Paralyzed with shame, she allowed her fluids to spill over onto Liz's desk, all over her own hands and into her lap. Liz wiped Tai's nose and face then pressed several tissues into her hand to awaken her from her stupor.

Liz gently lifted Tai's chin, "You don't have to be ashamed. I will always love you no matter what."

There was just enough time to hold Tai for a few minutes, whisper a prayer, then send her on her way. God was gracious that way. He made sure Liz never had to rush Celia out of her office even when several personalities presented their stories in the same session.

Hello Eliza,

I'm Tai. Celia Sue called me today. She said Jesus told her about your prayer today. She isn't mad at you anymore, but she still isn't coming home. She and Celia Paul are in Vermont.

Celia Sue said when she saw Leigha smiling, she had to leave. She said we have to tell you our stories, not lies, but tell you what happened to us. She doesn't want to hear it. She said it makes her mad then I comfort us. Celia Sue said not to worry about comforting us. She didn't leave because of me. She left because she would try to stop us from telling you our stories, not lies.

Celia Sue said she went back to Vermont because that's the last place she was when she had fun. She's not coming back until all the little girls tell you what happened to them. She said she couldn't sit in the Conference Room and listen to the sad stories and see us cry.

Celia Paul is with Celia Sue. They are staying together. Celia Paul is praying quietly for her so she can be all right. The Lord told Celia Paul where to find Celia Sue. She wouldn't promise to call again. She called this time to tell me to be brave and not to worry about her. I told her I was brave this morning.

Celia Sue is proud of me. I told her that I love her, and I miss her. She said she misses me, too. I was so excited to talk to Celia Sue that I forgot to talk to Celia Paul.

I love you, Eliza. I have a good secret to tell you. After I was brave this morning, I went back to bed, but I didn't rock us to sleep neither did Angelica. I didn't comfort us either. I love you, Eliza.

Love, Tai

Liz punched two holes in the top of Tai's letter and placed it in Celia's folder with all the previous letters. She thanked God for his faithfulness because she realized Tai's ability to sleep without rocking or masturbating came only by his grace (God's ability working in us).

It seemed as though Wednesday dawned more quickly than usual. When Liz walked into the waiting room, she recognized Celia, but she didn't recognize her alter personality. Her hair had been cut into a boyish bob. Her demeanor was somewhat masculine, which matched her red double breasted suit and gold trim accented with a gold silk tie and a red Kangol hat that rested on her knee.

"Good Morning Celia. Have we been properly introduced?"

"No, we haven't. I am the flamboyant Celia Paul. The propensity to be ostentatious comes from being so young and recognized for my sincerity and commitment to the Lord. It also comes from escaping the pain, the abuse and the disappointments of the younger parts of me."

"Well, Celia Paul, welcome back from Vermont. How's Celia Sue?"

"She still has her fears especially since she has been having nightmares. I persuaded her to come home, but I had to promise she didn't have to be in the Conference Room. She will come and see you when she gets tired of waking up screaming in the middle of the night. I don't think that's going to be much longer. She's having them pretty regularly. Oh, before I forget, Tai asked me to thank you for her surprise. She especially loved the four white doves at the top carrying a red heart on the end of the ribbon. All of us love cards, but especially Tai."

"Tell her she's welcome, but I'm sure you didn't come today to talk about Celia Sue or Tai. How may I help you? What would you like to talk about?"

Celia Paul stared blankly at Liz. Perhaps he had made a mistake in coming. This wasn't as easy as he had hoped. He took a deep breath and prayed the words would somehow find a voice.

"I'm thirteen, and Daddy taught me how to drive. That was cool because my brothers didn't get to learn until they were fifteen. Daddy bought a brand new station wagon, and he let me drive that, too. Before long, he told me to turn onto the expressway. Boy, the traffic sure did move fast. I wasn't even afraid. Daddy had to tell me to slow down. He wouldn't let anyone ride with us either. It was always just the two of us.

Sometimes he would walk in my bedroom at four o'clock in the morning and call my name. Then he'd tell me to get dressed. He always whispered so Justina and Sally wouldn't wake up. He asked me if I could see. I always said, 'Yes, Sir,' because that meant he was going to let me drive. We would go to the Farmer's Market and wait until the farmers brought their produce to sell. We were always the first ones there. We had to wait almost an hour each time we went."

"Celia Paul, you're giving me a great deal of information and details, but I sense there is something you aren't telling me. Let me hold your hand. It's all right to tell me what happened when your father taught you how to drive."

"I want to tell you, but the words just won't come," he whispered.

"That's all right; you can tell me when you're ready. There is no rush. I'm here for you."

"No, no Eliza, I have to tell you today. If I leave without telling you, it will be too difficult to tell you later.

Daddy would take me to a secluded place with a lot of open space for driving. He let me drive for about fifteen minutes or so, then he would tell me where to park. When he got out, he put the back two rows of seats down. He said his reward for teaching me how to drive was for me to make him feel good. Then he would have sex with me. When we went to the Farmer's Market, we got there early so he could have sex with me. He said he treats me special because he loves me. And when you love someone, you want to make them feel good."

Celia Paul put his hands over his face and wept. He had no desire to catch Liz's eye. He knew she hated him. He made up his mind he wasn't going to come to Liz's office ever again.

Just then an amazing thing happened. Celia Paul felt Liz's arm envelope him as she whispered, "S-h-h-h, s-h-h-h, s-h-h-h, it wasn't your fault; it wasn't your fault. Thank you for being so brave. I love you, Celia Paul, and God loves you, too."

With that assurance, Celia Paul relaxed, then quietly slipped back into the Conference Room, and Tai took his place.

"Tai, I wish to speak with Elvira."

"How did you know it was me? I never even said a word."

"I know you, Young Lady, every chance you get you make an

appearance so you can get a hug. I'll give you a quick hug, then may I please talk with Elvira?"

"Hello Liz, why did you ask to see me? I'm content with letting everyone else have a turn."

"I know you are, but it has been some time since you wrote to me, and you promised one of these days you would come out of the Conference Room to meet me. I wanted to check to make sure you are all right even though God has intervened in your life and healed you. I don't want you to feel like you have to be strong. I'm here for you, too."

Liz bowed her head and prayed, gave Elvira a hug, then walked her back to the waiting room.

It took a week before Liz's wisdom developed fruit.

Dear Eliza,

Celia and I are not getting along. She doesn't understand me. She has absolutely no experience with teenagers. That horrible man I had as a father taught me how to drive for his own wicked purposes of course. But I know how to drive nonetheless. Celia always complains when I drive. I have been doing most of the driving these days. I drive like a teenager; I cannot possibly drive like her. Would you please tell her to get a life and leave me alone?

Another reason why she and I are not getting along is because she is so critical of me. She tells me things I already know. Her reminding me just makes me angrier. She doesn't have to tell me that I am angry with the world, especially with E. F. I am glad he's dead, and I hope he burns in hell for the hell he put me through. He raped me lots of times.

That's why I hate Nathan. Nathan and E. F. are alike. Ever since Celia got married, I have been afraid. Nathan walks up on me without notice, and I hate him for that. That's the same thing E. F. used to do. I hate Nathan for being in my bedroom. I hate Nathan for wanting to have sex. I can satisfy my own sexual desires. I don't want any man touching me ever again. I hate Nathan because he puts his nasty tongue in my mouth. And if Celia thinks she is going to shout into "Heaven" dragging me along, she has another thing coming.

I know you and Ray are my new parents, but I won't forget about all my pain just like that, Mom. During your joint marriage session, I didn't feel angry with Nathan because I felt safe with you there. Then ole Celia came back and laid her head on his shoulder and felt content. That made me want to puke. I plan to be in control as often as I can so this kind of thing will not continue to happen.

Last week Nathan paid the first installment on burial plots. If he died right now, that would be just all right with me. Then he won't keep reminding me about that despicable three-legged person who provided the sperm for my existence.

With honesty,

Elvira, just Elvira

CHAPTER 5 ❖ DELIVERED FROM THE EVIL ONE

"My Lord is the Most High God. He is the King of Kings and the Lord of Lords. His name is Jesus, and his power within me is greater than you, Satan. You will not hurt, harm or influence Celia in any way." Liz spoke quietly, but firmly.

The Evil One influenced Celia to resist the name of Jesus. She jumped out of her chair and pressed her body against the wall. Yet, there was no escaping the powerful name of Jesus Christ.

"Satan, you must leave my office at once and appear before the throne of God."

When the release came, Celia's body slumped to the carpet.

"Were you coconscious; do you know what happened?"

"No, how did I end up on the floor?

"The enemy can not tolerate the name of Jesus. He influenced you to try to run. You leaned against the wall and cringed. As soon as

Satan left, your body slid to the floor.

Liz studied Celia's eyes. Her weariness communicated the need for a reprieve before traveling home. She gathered Celia's book, purse and coat, then escorted her to an unoccupied office. Celia lay down under her draped coat and went fast asleep.

An hour later Liz checked to see if Celia was rested, but found her motionless. She met with another client and visited her a second time. Celia had awakened. Liz talked with her; reassured she could make the journey home safely, she sent Celia on her way.

A loud piercing scream emanated from Liz's office and permeated the air throughout the corridor. It sent a chill down the spines of unsuspecting clients waiting for their appointments.

With a bit more intensity Liz exclaimed, "I am a child of the King; you have no choice but to submit to me, Satan. You will not use Celia's voice to scream, speak or utter a sound in my presence."

Immediately Celia put her hands over her ears. Determined to exercise the full power of God's authority Liz reached forward and pulled Celia's hands away.

"You will not dictate Celia's behavior. You have no right to trespass. You have no power to control, influence or impact Celia in any way. You must appear before the throne of God and obey his bidding."

As Liz began to work even more industriously the enemy manifested himself through various avenues. Celia acted out behaviors that were inconsistent with the person Liz had come to know, respect and love. Since spiritual warfare had now become a momumental concern. Liz further sought the Lord for his strategy for Celia's healing.

Aware that Satan used many weaknesses to gain access to Celia's brokenness, Liz paid strict attention to Celia's demeanor. Blatantly obvious that Satan was under foot Liz, began their next session with prayer.

"Well hello, Angelica. I haven't had the pleasure of talking

DELIVERED FROM THE EVIL ONE

with you for quite some time. I'm so glad you came today. I am going to read you a true story. At the end I hope you accept the special "gift" the story talks about."

Liz picked up The Picture Bible,[1] turned to the New Testament and read two short stories. The first title was "The Lord is Risen." The second title was "The Last Command." Angelica folded her arms to cradle her head. She loved listening to stories. She looked at the distinct red, green, blue and yellow hues as Liz turned each page. At the end, Liz introduced Angelica to the Lord Jesus Christ and rejoiced at Angelica's reception of Jesus into her heart.

Liz felt led to introduce Angelica to the Lord. Celia's personalities could not use the name of Jesus because they were affected by the enemy. In fact, they hated the name of Jesus. Liz believed if she could persuade Celia's family to invite Jesus into their hearts, then perhaps the real part of Celia could then be more able to join her in the fight for freedom and wholeness. It came as no surprise when The Evil One launched an all out attack on Liz, Celia and the many selves into which she was fragmented.

Good Morning Eliza,

    Some strange things have been happening. When I woke up my finger was hurting. It has a cut on it. I didn't have the cut before I went to sleep. There have been other occasions when I have awakened and found scratches on my arm.

    What is happening to me? Am I going to be all right? Why am I getting cuts and scratches I can't explain? Help me please Eliza; I don't know what to do. Please call me. I need you. I will try to be patient, but can you please call me today?

Love, C. C.

Ring, ring, ring, "Hello."
"Hello Celia, this is Marcie from Liz's office. I'm calling to

cancel your appointment for Monday. Liz was hit by a car last evening. She was treated and released from the hospital, but she will not be back to work by Monday. I will give you a call to reschedule. Liz wanted me to tell you she will be all right so you don't have to worry."

Anxiety disrupted Celia's entire family. Tai started running through the house screaming and crying. She made everybody tired. When she finally calmed down, Angelica went in the room to get Pooh, and Celia Kid sucked her thumb while knotting her hair. This was devastating news. Celia had no idea how to function without Liz.

Ring, ring, ring, "Hello."

"Hello Tai, I called to let you know I will be all right. I know you wanted to it hear it from me rather than from Marcie. I'm pretty sore and bruised. I was walking across the parking lot and was hit by a Crown Victoria. Those are very sturdy cars.

I want you to take your medicine to calm yourself. You can expect a brief call from me each day. I want to know how you are doing, and you will know that I am feeling better. I will try to get back to work part-time as soon as possible. Hopefully, I will be absent only a week. You will be one of the first clients I see. How will that be?"

"That will be great. I'll talk with you tomorrow. I love you Eliza. Thank you for being my mom and calling me. Good bye."

First, the inexplicable cuts and scratches alerted Liz that The Evil One was physically attacking Celia actually causing her to create self-inflicted wounds. Second, her accident indicated they were in the midst of satanic warfare. Though Satan's attacks could not be ignored, Liz had assurance that El Shaddai's mighty power would prevail. Celia's healing *would* come. Reassurance of that truth came in the mail.

Dear Eliza,

Nathan took me to my doctor's appointment because Celia had to see if she has a permanent disability. I don't want anybody taking you away from me. I love you, and I don't want to talk with anybody else but you.

    Eliza, can I ask Jesus into my heart like Angelica did? Angelica still wants to see you again, but she says she has Jesus in her heart and she likes for Jesus to be in her heart. Now Angelica can leave Pooh at home, but I still carry Snuggles.

    That's why the doctor was mean to me. I carried Snuggles with me, but I didn't do anything wrong. I answered all her questions, and I cried when she said I have a severe problem. She asked Nathan if he leaves me at home by myself as if I were a little baby. She made me mad.

    Please don't let her take me away from you, Eliza, please, please, please. I love you Eliza.

Love to Eliza, From Tai

    Liz kept her word and talked briefly with Celia each day. Within a week, she returned to work part-time. The threats of the enemy did not deter Liz. She continued to follow the prompting of God's Holy Spirit at every stage of Celia's healing process.

Dear Eliza,

    Celia Paul asked me to thank you for introducing him to Jesus Christ. He will send you a Thank You card tomorrow and express his gratitude when he meets with you again.

    We had quite a session on Friday. Celia would like for you to tell her what happened because she doesn't know. I wasn't able to tell her. All she knows is four of us accepted the Lord Jesus Christ as our Savior. By the way, *thank you very much for showing me how to ask Jesus into my heart.* Although nothing has changed, I feel different somehow. Maybe the full release will come when I tell you my story.

    Eliza, may I please have today's session? I am willing to share the last ten minutes with Celia because I realize it's important for her to know what goes on in our sessions. She feels uncomfortable when she is aware something significant happened, but isn't fully sure what actually transpired.

Even though I asked Jesus into my heart, I'm still angry. I am angry with Cordella for leaving me at the altar with that man. She is the one who decided to marry him not me. She walked down the aisle so she should have been the one walking up the aisle rather than skipping out and leaving me stuck with a husband I didn't ask for or want.

She says she's at peace, but I'm definitely not at peace with her. I feel she owes me an apology. How can she be so cruel and act like everything is all right? Sometimes I feel like I hate her! Her pain is the reason why I am a sinful woman. She could have at least selected someone who is fun to be with or has some interests.

He doesn't associate with anybody. He seldom goes anywhere; when he does, he's usually back within a two-hour period. His life is filled with television as though it has become his idol, his captor and his very life's blood. Perhaps it is Satan's way of stalemating him to keep the marriage from ever being supportive and gratifying.

I'm angry because I got stuck with this man and this marriage. I want out! Do you hear me, Eliza? I want out of this horrible marriage. I didn't ask to be a part of Celia or this family. I don't want to be married. I want to be single like the rest of my sisters and brothers. I want out of this miserable marriage. Do you hear me, Eliza? I want out right now!

That's all I have to say because I am angry. I'm angry with you; I'm angry with Cordella; I am angry with myself, and I am definitely angry with that knucklehead of a husband, Nathan.

It's, C. Colleenii B.

During their months of joint sessions, Liz knew Nathan to be a godly man who loved his wife dearly. It was extremely difficult for him to live with the many personalities claiming Celia's life. She knew The Evil One had infiltrated every aspect of their marriage where he could get a *toehold*. God's grace and protection, however, prevented him from gaining a *foothold*. Through those eyes, Liz understood C. Colleenii B.'s letter and prayed for wisdom to handle it gingerly.

As Liz sought the Lord's wisdom, she became keenly aware that the Celia she now knew was unlike the Celia she had been seeing. Pride, a key demonic influence, wreaked havoc on Celia's being; she became non-relational, arrogant, stern and surly. Guilt and shame prevented direct eye contact with Liz.

To be delivered from The Evil One became Liz's number one priority in her prayers for Celia. All parts of Celia related to her on some level, but there were distinct traits that existed outside Celia Canterbury's true personality. During those times, some true alter personality would have struggles with some unwanted behavior including manifestations of hatred and bitterness.

Liz had learned that Satan gained access when boundaries are breached in a young child; the child has no way to distinguish what is truth and what is not. Celia's own boundaries had been breached for nearly fifty years. For that same length of time, Satan's influence had hovered over Celia's life.

Liz determined to lead each personality into a saving knowledge of Jesus Christ. To win this battle, she required not only God's strength, but Celia's ability and willingness to join in the struggle.

Hi Eliza,

I got to see you two times this week. That was fun, but the reason wasn't fun. I'm going to say my prayers when I go to bed tonight because I promised and the angels are going to be on top of my house and at the windows and all the doors.

Eliza, I forgot that you don't like for me to be ashamed of myself and hold my head down because Jesus is up and not down, huh, Eliza? I like it when you lift my head with your finger. One day I will remember not to be ashamed of myself and put my head down. Thank you for letting me ask Jesus into my heart. Maybe he will help me not to be ashamed if I ask him.

    C. C. gets to see you on Friday. She said I can come with her, but Snuggles and Pooh have to stay home. I said, "Okay" because I wanted to come and not stay at home. Guest what, Eliza? I didn't comfort us since Monday. I let Nathan hold us.

    Eliza, I take more medicine now. Will we have to do more work and clean up better because of the medicine and not have bad thoughts? I'm sorry, Eliza, that I made you sad today. No more bad thoughts about hurting myself or Nathan. You told the devil to go away and leave me alone. I promised; so if I have any more bad thoughts, I will not do anything bad, I will just tell you about it and you can chase the devil away again, huh Eliza?

    C. C. said not to write a long letter for you to have to read during her time. She said she gave me two days with you, let me ride on the scooter, and she read me a story, that's enough. So bye, Eliza. I love you.

Love, Tai

    The mystery of working with Celia was the reality that painful information existed outside the recollection of the other members of Celia's system of personalities. Liz had the delicate responsibility of communicating potentially excruciating information.

"Good morning, Tai. It's nice to see you. Today, I have to have Celia here."

"Good morning, Eliza. Tai was pouting, but she will get over it. She said you wanted to meet with me today. What's up?"

"Celia Sue told me something that you need to know. She said you and Osmund had an inappropriate relationship."

"How do I know she was telling you the truth?"

"She said you pounded his head on the basement floor because you almost got caught. Do you remember that?"

"I remember pounding his head, but I never remembered why."

"I believe she supplied that piece of the puzzle."

"What did we do that was inappropriate?"

"Celia Sue did not give any specific details. She said that you loved Osmund more than any of your other siblings and that the two of you did things that a brother and sister aren't supposed to do."

"Did Osmund and I have sex?"

"She didn't say that."

Liz was deliberate in telling Celia her own story. It was time to introduce Celia to the truth that the sexual abuse happened to her. Sooner or later she had to embrace the fact that all the personalities were just one person, Celia herself. This was the first time Liz had been prompted by God's Holy Spirit to make that distinction. It did not escape Celia's recognition.

Celia looked at Liz with an expression she had never seen before. Stunned and in shock Celia said nothing more. It was as though she had been suspended in time and incapable of movement.

Liz waited for a moment for Celia's response. None presented itself so she said, "Now would be a good time for a hug."

As Liz leaned forward Celia stretched her body in the opposite direction. Then she mechanically stood up and walked stiffly to the window. Her head leaned against the windowsill while her mouth stood ajar. The thick silence hung a cloud of doom over the entire office. Liz stood behind Celia not knowing what behavior her emotions would dictate. Steadily and slowly Celia's body began to slide down the wall. When she realized Celia was fainting, she gently supported her body to break her fall.

Celia's head plopped on her left arm while her legs folded in a fetal position. For a while she was lifeless. Suddenly, Celia began to moan and weep. She screamed with a velocity that had reached into the very depths of her being for exposure. Her hands constricted with such force they scrawled a pattern on the carpet. Fluids ran from her nose and mouth and met her tears that created a puddle on the floor.

There were no words of comfort. There were no songs to sing in her ear as Liz had done so many times before. There were no stories to read. There were no Bible verses to recite that would ease Celia's pain. Liz knelt down, pressed a handful of tissues into Celia's palm, laid her face against Celia's cheek and cried with her.

Dear Eliza,

    I need to understand what is happening to me, and how you know I am going to be all right. I'm worried, Eliza. I am worried. I want so much to believe you, but there is a part of me that is suffering from a serious case of the doubts.

    This week for the first time in a long time I asked myself, "If you were going to commit suicide, what method would you use?" Eliza, I don't think this is a problem, but you may give it a different perspective. I decided I wanted to die peacefully so I probably would take an overdose of one of my prescriptions.

    Believe me, Eliza, I'm not thinking about committing suicide. I'm not even sure why that question popped into my head. Maybe it's because of our last session and Celia Sue had another automobile accident yesterday. She doesn't know how to drive, but she keeps getting behind the wheel.

    I had the presence of mind to call my oldest brother. I was crying and afraid of the police. Pete took care of everything. I made it back home without too big of an emotional scene. Perhaps I am learning how to fight against Satan's attacks after all. I hope so.

Love, Celia

    Despite Liz's faith and resolve, Satan devised several strategies to sabotage Celia's healing process. Because Celia was a connoisseur of fine literature, she purchased <u>The Handbook of Spiritual Warfare</u>[2] and began reading. Liz innocently encouraged Celia to bring the book for her perusal. After leafing through the pages, she announced her intentions to keep it. Liz was unwilling to allow the enemy to use information from the book against Celia's best interest since she had a strong desire to be in charge. There were personalities who had yet to be introduced to Jesus Christ so Satan still had access. Determined not to give The Evil One a clue of her therapeutic plan to bring him under control, Liz forbade Celia to purchase or read any books without her approval.

When Satan failed in using <u>The Handbook of Spiritual Warfare</u> to destroy Celia, he introduced an alter that was not a personality. Wellington paraded as an alter for quite some time. He was clever in his presentation of himself. Therefore, it wasn't immediately clear that he wasn't a part of Celia. Satan was cunning and also spoke to Celia. After all, she did have two other masculine personalities. Yet, there were things about Wellington that deviated from Celia's true personalities.

There wasn't a single letter written by Wellington among the hundreds Liz had already received. He made his appearance after six of Celia's personalities accepted Jesus Christ. He asked Celia to give him a name rather than receiving a name from Celia consistent with her recollections of various experiences during a particular time in her life. Liz felt no sense of relationship with Wellington even though he presented in her office on several occasions.

Liz realized that arrogance characterized many of Celia's thought processes, but Wellington seemed to consistently display an abundance of that attitude. Too often he was confused about details that had already been established.

As Liz noticed these variations she began to consult professional literature for possible explanations. This was critical because she was going to be out of town over the next ten days. Much to her delight she found helpful insight. She began devouring <u>Uncovering the Mystery of MPD</u>[3]. Liz thanked God for the chart that supplied her with the help she needed.

Discerning Alter Personalities From Demons[4]

Alter Personality	Demon
1. Most alters, even "Persecutor" alters, can become strong allies. There is a definite sense of relationship with them, even if it starts out negative.	1. Demons are arrogant, and there is no sense of relationship with them.
2. Alters initially seem ego-dystonic but that changes to be ego-syntonic over time.	2. Demons remain ego-alien-- "outside of me."
3. Confusion and fear subside with appropriate therapy when only alters are present.	3. Confusion, fear and lust persist despite therapy when demons are present.
4. Alters tend to conform to surroundings.	4. Demons force unwanted behavior, then blame a personality.
5. Alters have personalities with accompanying voices.	5. Demons have a negative voice which has no corresponding personality.
6. Irritation, discontent and rivalry abound among alters.	6. Hatred and bitterness are the common feelings among demons.
7. Images of alters are human in form, and remain consistent during imagery.	7. The imagery of demons changes between human and non-human forms, with many variations.

    Satan relentlessly pursued his attempts to destroy Celia. He had no intention of allowing her to survive so he put his next plan into action. He thought since Liz was out of town, he would appeal to her husband, Ray, who worked with Celia jointly with Nathan and in Liz's absence.

DELIVERED FROM THE EVIL ONE

Dearest Ray,

Please allow me to introduce myself. I am Penelope P. Pembrooke. I am an accomplished writer and speaker. I am a Bostonian by birth and breeding. It was not my intention to interfere with the struggles of the Abernathy-Canterbury family, but Celia was having such a difficult time dealing with being a multiple that I just couldn't sit back and not give her a helping hand.

Celia created me as a pseudonym for her writing. I have been as patient with her as I possibly can. She isn't getting her housework completed; she fails to allow Tai to practice her piano lessons; she has done simply awful with C. C.'s exercise and nutrition program; so I suggested she take a sabbatical.

She decided to go to Vermont and revisit a more serene time in her life. I think that was an excellent choice. There is hope for her yet. She didn't go alone; Gwendolynn is with her. Gwendolynn spent two summers there attending school. She will be the best companion for Celia.

Ray, this letter purposes not to be very long. The reason why Celia is taking a vacation is because she dreamed that Osmund was alive and interacting with various people. Osmund is dead, but she refuses to accept that fact. She also comforted us twice yesterday. I know Liz will be disappointed that she won't be able to talk with Celia for a while; however, I truly believe mine was a good decision. See you tomorrow.

Truly yours,

Penelope P. Pembrooke

Ray received yet a second letter showing that Celia's absence was impeding her healing.

Dear Ray,

I need help; when is Liz coming home? I don't know who I am; I haven't been sleeping, and I have been forgetting to take my medicine. I'm lost and confused; when is Liz coming home?

Penelope is gone. She left sometime on Wednesday afternoon.

Celia is still in Vermont. She hasn't called or written since she left. Would you please ask Liz to call me and to please come home today? I'm falling apart. I don't like it when I don't know who I am.

Ray, when is Liz coming home? Do you think she will be safe and come home well? I don't know what I am going to do without Liz. I need her. She will know who I am or she will help me discover who I am. I don't like being a person without a name. Thank you for helping me and telling Liz what I said.

Honestly, Whoever I Am

Ring, ring, ring, "Hello."

"Hello Celia Sue, please ask everyone to come to the Conference Room. I have an important message."

"Celia isn't here. She went to Vermont. We don't know what to do without her. When are you coming home?"

"Soon, but listen up. I was in prayer this morning and the Lord told me to call you to deliver this message. *I will never lose track of you. I will never lose track of who you are.*"

"Oh, Eliza, thank you for calling and telling us. Please tell Ray thank you for delivering our message to you."

"I haven't spoken to Ray today. He didn't tell me to call you; God did. The Lord knew you were troubled so he asked me to call and reassure you of his love. Try not to worry about Celia. I will pray she returns quickly. I'm confident she will probably be home by the time I get back. I will see you on Monday."

"Bye Eliza. Thank you for calling us, and we will try not to worry. I hope the next four days go by really fast."

Monday greeted both Liz and Celia for another hard day's work. As it had become their custom, Liz began by reading a letter.

Dear Eliza,

I was bad yesterday and C. C. gave me a bubble bath and put me in the bed. She said I made everybody tired because I was running through the house and screaming and crying. I saw Andy and I was afraid he was going to try to pull my panties down again.

C. C. said you might give me more medicine. Sunday I wanted to take lots and lots of medicine, but Nathan said, "No." I was afraid of Andy so I just wanted to sleep and sleep and sleep and sleep so he can't hurt me anymore.

Pooh and Snuggles took care of me yesterday. When Andy tried to come into the house from the basement Pooh said he will kick him in the balls. Snuggles said he would bite him in the butt. Is that bad to say, Eliza? Anyway, Andy must have left because Pooh and Snuggles said I could go downstairs and Andy wasn't down there anymore, and I'm glad.

Love, Tai

This kind of confusion became Satan's next strategy. Liz continued to meet with each personality and allowed them to make the decision to ask Jesus Christ into their hearts. Liz found that she had the privilege of working with more true personality parts. There was less resistance to the name of Jesus. Celia wasn't as confused or irritated. She began to function better at home with cooking and keeping her house clean. Nevertheless, The Evil One tried once again to sabotage Celia's recovery.

Liz walked to the waiting room to get Celia. Sitting across from the door was a stately woman wearing an authentic African outfit. It was elaborate and quite colorful with a distinct pattern sewn with a gorgeous orangish-yellow glow. Its beauty adorned the neck, the sleeves and the bottom of both the blouse and the skirt.

"Hello Liz, my name is Imani. Imani means faith. It's so nice to have this auspicious occasion to meet with you."

The arrogance she exuded left no doubt that Satan was masquerading once again as an impostor. Liz didn't even hesitate.

"Satan, how dare you show up in my office. You will in no uncertain terms confuse, influence, hurt or harm Celia in any way whatsoever. By the power of God's Holy Spirit in me and through the blood of Jesus and by the authority of his name, I command you to appear before the throne of God. If you don't obey me at once, God will send you to the fire before your time. Go. Now."

Liz spoke more adamantly than before because there was only one more person to accept the Lord Jesus Christ. That was Celia, herself. She had no intentions of the enemy disrupting her plans.

Friday, October third etched its signifigance on the corridors of Celia's heart. There were no more voices. There were no more selves into which Celia had been fragmented.

Pooh, Snuggles and all the stuffed animals that rode in Celia's car were placed in a large bag and handed over to Liz months ago. Angelica and Celia Kid no longer sucked their thumbs or knotted their hair in nervous degradation. The uncontrollable shaking and rocking subsided. The confusion and the overt satanic warfare came to a screeching halt. There was no more rootin' tootin' cowboy or a masculine preacher, Celia Paul. Although she still called her Eliza, Liz had now become Celia's coach.

Celia Colleen Canterbury had finally become an adult player on life's stage. She desperately needed a coach. Celia had absolutely no idea how to live and function as an individual. Tai no longer housed her anxieties. Celia Sue no longer managed her anger. C. C. relinquished her weight loss program, and C. Colleenii B. passed the baton of marriage.

A mother and a daughter traveled a long and arduous journey to an emotional oneness. The time had finally come for a coach and an athlete to enter the arena of emotional and spiritual maturity.

CHAPTER 6 ❖ THE SILHOUETTE OF A PRINCESS

Dear Eliza,
    I am Celia Colleen Abernathy and I hate Janna Cherie Abernathy. I have been afraid of her all my life. Tai was allowed to spend the night with Janna Cherie because I wanted a mom so badly that I was willing to pretend that my birth mother was finally capable of loving me since she acted like a mom after my automobile accident.
    Truthfully, I was using Tai. I kept hoping Janna Cherie would die while Tai was there. I thought maybe there was some way to help the process along. I want to be the one to discover her body. I want her to die before she gets her final check from Osmund's profit sharing. She was named the beneficiary; I am the secondary beneficiary. If she dies before the check comes, it's mine. I deserve it for all the *hell* I put up with from her. Every time I call her and let the telephone ring, I'm hoping she's in the house dead. I am disappointed when she an-

swers the phone.

If there was some way for me to get rid of her without breaking the law, I would. I hate her, but not enough to ruin my life for killing her. Sometimes I wish she would cough herself to death. I wish her cancer would finally destroy her. She's had it for twenty-six years. Why is it taking so long for the disease to finish her off?

Don't worry, Eliza, I won't be sleeping over at Janna Cherie's house anymore. I really don't have to, you know. I have her house keys, her car keys (which is in my name by the way), her checking, savings and a CD have my name on it. All those things are automatically mine when she dies. I want everything she can possibly give to compensate for refusing to defend me when I needed her most.

I have been nothing but a wonderful daughter to her (not perfect, but wonderful), but that never was enough for Janna Cherie. Maybe she's sorry that she was unsuccessful in her attempt to abort me when I was growing inside her those many years ago. The day she dies will be a happy day for me, and I hope that's real soon. I would even be willing to miss a session with you to attend her funeral. On second thought, no I wouldn't.

Janna Cherie doesn't want a funeral anyway. She only wants a memorial ceremony. Actually, I don't care what she has. I just want to look into her face and verify for myself that she is finally dead. I may not even go to the memorial service. My reason would be my own. Forty-nine years is way too long to live in a fantasy world of pretending to love her. I'm through pretending.

Well Eliza, I think this letter will go down in history as a turning point in my life. We will see.

Relinquishing duplicity,

Celia Colleen Abernathy Canterbury

Liz didn't have to wait and see. The letter demonstrated Celia owned her hatred for her mother. She gave her a clear picture of the immediate work that awaited them. Fully understanding the complexity of Celia's mind and her appreciation for the power of words, God prompted Liz to share a phenomenal literary piece she had written.

Landscape Metaphor[1]

Once a landscape that was beautifully created, lush and fertile was ravaged by a great storm so that it left a crater where little could grow. The gaping scar was painful and the owner of the landscape threw a tarp over it hoping no one would notice. Unfortunately, under the tarp the remnants of the grasses and beautiful flowers completely died in the dark and dank crater. Various pestilences began to grow and further eroded the crater and began to restructure the whole area beneath the tarp so that it didn't resemble what its Designer had created.

The owner would periodically check to see that the tarp stayed in place and even threw some artificial grass on top and placed artificial flowers around it in order to further hide the scarred landscape. The owner began to look at the tarp as though it were real, but took no joy in it because the flowers gave off no fragrance since they weren't real. The artificial turf didn't feel refreshing on her bare feet.

Several times the wind blew a corner of the tarp up and some additional erosion occurred. Then the owner began to feel ill because the landscape that was meant to sustain her was failing to do so.

The owner went to a gardener trained by the Designer of the landscape who began to slowly remove the artificial planting and assured the owner that the Designer had a plan to totally recreate the landscape in a way she could not imagine. The owner could hardly believe that because she had forgotten how horrible the crater beneath really was and had not known it had been filled with debris and disease over the years.

The gardener persisted, however, and gently convinced her to let her slowly pull back the tarp so the Designer could do what he had longed to do all the time. She promised to be right there when the crater was cleaned out and then refilled with the fertile, rich, life-giving soil that the Designer would use to recreate the lush landscape.

The owner had known the Designer for a long time, but never knew what he had created in her at the beginning when he had spoken her into existence. She trembled at the thought of being exposed with all the barren spots so visible. As the gardener began to clear away the debris and disease that had attached itself, it seemed exceedingly painful. The gardener continued, however, and reassured her it would be beautiful beyond her dreams one day and she slowly cleaned the crater and brought in the soil of the Designer wherever he told her to do so.

Be of good cheer. The Designer is an Award Winner and has turned rock into gushing water, made food from a barren landscape, turned water into wine and created a celestial city with streets of gold and gates made of a single pearl. Certainly it is not too difficult to recreate a crater!

Liz, M.S., LPCC
Marriage & Family Therapist

Celia understood the Landscape Metaphor. Pleased Eliza had given her perspective on the debris under her tarp, Celia determined to face the task head-on. She agreed that Liz's work as the gardener would be painful, but nonetheless delicate and purposeful.

She had thought becoming a whole person was the most difficult part of her journey. Facing the reality of clearing away the debris and disease the sexual abuse had impressed upon her life and relationships presented Celia with an even greater challenge. She knew it was time to start with her deepest pain, then move forward.

"Celia, your letter exuded extreme hatred. I can't begin to imagine what your childhood was like. I just know that if you will trust God and me, it is possible to have a loving adult relationship with your mother."

"That woman had to know something was terribly wrong. Don't you remember when I sent you several paragraphs from my short story entitled *The Secret?*"

> Overt signs began to manifest themselves. Little by little bald spots appeared where thick, curly, coal black hair had once brought glory. An uncontrollable shaking could have rocked a crying baby fast asleep. Blood curdling screams pierced the night and startled the entire household into wakening. Didn't anyone suspect that something was wrong -- dreadfully wrong? Her once beautiful locks of hair became knots as she pulled and curled the strands in nervous degradation of keeping a secret, participating in the secret and living the secret herself.

Celia raised her voice, "I hate her because she must have known, but she never did anything about it. She just ignored it and pretended like it wasn't happening. I hate her; I have always hated her, and I see no reason to stop now."

"Sh-h-h, sh-h-h, sh-h-h. Close your eyes. Take a deep breath. Imagine you are walking along the banks of a rippling brook. You can hear the water as it gently trips and falls over stones while it flows down stream. A quiet breeze makes the branches of a giant oak tree bow and wave in the distance. Sitting under the tree is a man beckoning you to come and sit with him. He wants to embrace and comfort you. The man is Jesus."

"Oh no, no, no," Celia screamed as she covered her face and began to cry.

"I can't go to Jesus. He doesn't want anything to do with me. I'm too despicable. I'm tainted goods. Don't you understand? Daddy said when you love someone you have sex with that person. He never told me that it mattered if any partner was a man *or* a woman. Jesus doesn't love me because I practiced what Daddy taught me. He is too holy. He would never want to spend time with me. Sitting by the brook with Jesus is something I'll never be able to do."

There was no reasoning with Celia so Liz didn't even try. She rolled her chair closer to her client and held her in a warm embrace. For now, all she could do was demonstrate the matchless love of Jesus Christ.

Liz never stopped being amazed how faithfully the Lord manifested himself at each stage of therapy. As she prepared for their next session she realized they would begin discussing Chapter Twelve of Sandra Wilson's book <u>Released from Shame: Recovery for Adult Children of Dysfunctional Families</u>.[2] The chapter title *"Released to Forgive the Shamers"* would meet Celia's desire to move forward in her healing process.

"Well Dr. C, Good Morning. I especially prayed for you over the weekend that God would give you a calming spirit as you read Chapter Twelve."

"Thank you, Eliza, I really needed it. For the first time I felt that maybe one day I will be able to forgive my mother and let go of this deep hatred."

"What part of the chapter gave you hope?"

"There were two parts. The first one was the *Reasons to Forgive*, 1) I have been born into God's family by his grace, 2) When I become more like God, I will benefit my earthly family, and 3) Forgiveness allows me to focus on the future rather than the past.[3]

The second part was the *Misunderstandings about Forgiveness*, 1) Forgiveness means nothing ever happened or that it was "no big deal," 2) Forgiving means automatic, instant, unlimited reconciliation, and 3) Forgiving means never having any painful memories or emotions related to the hurts or the hurters."[4]

I thought you just wanted me to forget all my pain, act like it was no big deal and forgive Janna Cherie without validating my feelings. I just have to keep remembering that I can do anything through God's strength."

Over the next several months and into the following year Liz began to see a more pronounced silhouette of the beauty in Celia's life. Her next task was to further encourage Celia to live with a greater dependence on God.

Suspended somewhere between relinquishing a mom for a coach and a lesser dependence on Liz for a greater dependence on God, Celia struggled with the daily demands of life. Her letter manifested her private thoughts.

My dearest Daddy-God,

Good Evening, this is Celia. I love you so much. The more I learn of you, the more I love you. You have gone to great lengths to protect me from myself and The Evil One. Thank you. I am now learning how to have a Daddy who loves me, cares for me and who has plans for me to prosper. I am learning how to depend on a Daddy who will not harm me, but whose plans are to give me a hope and a future.

This is difficult for me because all I have known from human relationships is pain, more pain and excruciating pain especially from E. F. Because of that particular relationship, I struggle with the ability to approach you as Daddy. At this very moment I need you to hold me and comfort me because my precious heart has been broken in two and tainted by my earthly parents.

I don't even know how to embrace your comfort that can fill the void I am carrying from the pain in my past. When I am hurting, my first inclination is to turn to Eliza. Today, for the first time I realize that she has always taken me by the hand and led me straight to you.

What Eliza wants me to hide in my heart is, "You, Daddy, are the source of *all* things." The love she gives me comes from you. The comfort Eliza gives me comes from you. Everything she has given me comes from you to her to me. Her prayer continues to be that I, myself, can and will go directly to the "source" to receive from you all that I need.

Thank you for Eliza. I know it's time to let go of the grip lock I have on her hand and hold yours ever so tighty. I know now that my first priority is to call on you from now on. Then when I need your love, care, protection and comfort to be clothed in human flesh, you will allow Eliza to be your ambassador.

Lord, right now I loosen my grip on Eliza's hand, and I tighten my clasp of your hand. Enpower me to look ever to Jesus keeping my eyes, my heart, my will and every desire fixed upon him.

Daddy, please wrap your arms around me and comfort me until the mending of my heart is complete. Please tear down all the barriers that hinder me from fully knowing you as "Abba Father." Replace them with gates of thanksgiving that surrounds your courts of praise. Be my strength everyday, hour by hour, minute by minute, moment by moment. Make me, Lord, a pillar of spiritual strength and fortitude as I fasten my spiritual armour more securely. Let victory reign within the very recesses of my being as I march onward and upward fulfilling your call upon my life as a Minister of the Gospel of Jesus Christ.

> Your humble servant,
>
> Celia C. Canterbury

◆╂ ◆╂ ◆╂ ◆╂ ◆╂

Five years had walked across the corridors of therapy, and Celia began to face her greatest challenges. For the first time in forty-seven years she was a whole person. What other fifty-year-old women face presented a mystery to Celia. Liz quietly moved into her role as a coach guiding Celia's choices, decisions and journey to emotional and spiritual maturity.

A portion of their sessions covered personal hygiene, choosing a hair stylist for a becoming appearance, wearing make-up, scheduling manicures and pedicures. Celia brought in various feminine items, and Liz explained their purpose and how to use them. Secretly Celia emulated Eliza. She wanted to be just like her. It didn't matter that Liz wasn't African American; it was her intelligence, her inner and outer beauty that spoke volumes to Celia.

Liz's fingernails were always neat and clean and every strand of her hair was in place. Celia watched how Eliza sat in her chair, the way she laughed and how she interacted with her husband, Ray, when they were in joint sessions. Celia was learning how to become a mature woman from her observations of Liz's godly mannerisms and relationships. She was intrigued by her petite size and dainty ways. If she could only be like Eliza, Celia felt her life would be complete.

To be like Liz, however, was not God's desire for Celia. He had a plan and a purpose that only Celia could fill with her own style and effervescence. That was a painful revelation to face. The Lord began to speak tenderly and deliberately as he allowed Celia to struggle with her perception of Liz, herself and the shaping of her immediate present and future.

Dear Eliza,

Ever since yesterday, I have been trying to make sense out of what is happening to me. I woke up in the middle of the night and immediately starting masturbating. It was like a boulder that had been picking up momentum stumbling down the hillside. I woke up the instant it reached the bottom, and I was bolted into a conquered (I thought) and forgiven behavior.

To identify the boulder becomes the critical challenge. The boulder has many rough and rugged edges. The nucleus is being an emotional newborn blanketed in a half-century crib with a third grade reference library of immature feelings and expressions. Another edge is my inability to verbalize my experiences without directly correlating them to my many personalities.

I'm trying to make sense out of my behavior. Thank you for spending an extra hour with me. I vacillate between not believing in myself and trusting God to see me through this. When I do well, it's so easy to believe. When I am human, it's so easy to disbelieve.

Becoming human is my problem and fear. All my life I have had reliable personalities to switch at will to accomplish what needed to be completed at any given time. I also believe each alter helped the other when it was needed, thus allowing me to handle so much. I had begun to believe that I was invincible. Learning I am human seems to be producing problems right now.

I am feeling rather overwhelmed at the moment -- knowing it isn't God's will for me to become like you, but to discover the person he created me to be. Soooooooo, I am eating and eating and eating all the wrong things, all the wrong times, and all the wrong amounts. Eliza, will I ever overcome my food and sexual addictions?

Deep in my heart I honestly believe I really haven't accomplished very much at all. When everything is said and done and I'm still out of shape, overweight, and undesirable to myself, I will feel what was the use anyway. If I can't be totally whole, what is the benefit of being partially whole. In my estimation "having no stick" is better than having "half a stick."

Well, that's my sad commentary for tonight. It's a good thing God's mercies are new every morning. What would I do without his faithfulness?

With love, Celia

Liz took Celia right back to their work with Pat Springle's book, <u>Trusting: Learning Who and How to Trust Again</u>.[5] Going back to the basics became critical to moving forward.

"Celia, do you remember what we discussed about trusting and self-confidence? Take a moment and reflect."

"Pat Springle said, 'Authentic self-confidence involves a true appraisal of my strengths and weaknesses which is the opposite of ego-centered pride. Knowing my limitation does not equal shame, and being confident in my abilities does not parallel pride.'[6] But I hate to admit my weaknesses."

"Meditate on those words. There is something else he wrote that would be helpful, 'As a loving and wise Father, God knows just how much to encourage us by using our strengths and how much to humble us by exposing our sinfulness and failures.'[7] God wants to draw you closer to him."

"I do want to be strong and mature. A lot of times I still feel like I'm eight year old Tai. I do want to overcome every despicable behavior associated with the abuse."

"Don't be so hard on yourself. Growth takes time. You can begin to look at your circumstance in a more positive light and to work more sincerely. There are times when I think you feel your life would be easier if you were still a multiple."

Celia took Liz's admonition to heart. The days, weeks and months turned into years of intense therapy as Liz and Celia worked diligently to recreate the lush landscape of Celia's life. She struggled with her addictions, but began to see glimpses of discipline from time to time. There were occasions, however, when Celia didn't try as hard to overcome the difficulties she faced. Liz knew she had to be true to God's calling to provide spiritual guidance. That task was sometimes as painful for her as it was for Celia.

My dearest Eliza,

You sure beat me up today, and in no uncertain terms delivered my comeupance. I was so wounded I needed medical attention so I went to the Heavenly Hospital to make an appointment with Jesus the Great Physician.

I didn't have to wait; he took me right in. I told him my sister Eliza beat me up today with capital "T" Truth and made deep cuts in my arrogance and pride with the Sword of the Spirit. Doctor Jesus said, "I ordained her to do that today because she loves you dearly, and I love you even more." He also said that he appreciates how the three of us have been working so diligently and steadfastly to restore my lush and fertile landscape, but I had become dead weight (every pun intended). I was sitting down and had stopped fighting the enemy on this issue of my addictions, especially my weight, hating my appearance and myself.

Doctor Jesus told me that he forgives me and has given me the power to overcome my addictions. He reminded me that the food addiction isn't as entrenched as the sexual addiction, which I had for forty-five years. This one is only about fifteen years old.

Before I left his office, he gave me a prescription. When I take my medication in the morning, say two prayers -- one for guidance and one for deliverance. Next I am to pray without ceasing throughout the day. When I take my medication at night, say two prayers -- one of thanksgiving and one of praise. The last thing Doctor Jesus said was, "All the other things would be added to you."

I love you so much, Eliza. Please thank Ray for taking the time to pray with you before our sessions, especially today.

                    Recovering nicely,   Celia

Each time Liz received a letter from Celia, she relinquished its contents to prayer. She may have been the gardener, but God indeed was the Designer who knew exactly his purpose for the shaping of Celia's life. With clear purpose, Liz began her next session with a plan.

"Celia, there is a Clinic that has an excellent Department of Nutrition Therapy. They have a program called "Eating Aware." Here's the name of an Endocronologist who will assign you to a registered dietitian to monitor your progress.

What do you think will be your greatest hindrance to being succesful with this program? Maybe we can strategize before you get started."

"The hardest thing for me is discipline. Each of my personalities exercised the freedom to appear whenever the need presented itself. So I find it an enormous challenge to discipline myself in this area of my life."

"You will be accountable to the dietitian on a weekly basis. That will provide one incentive. I'll tell you what. When you lose fifty pounds, I will spend a half a day with you outside the office."

Celia smiled and looked at Liz in disbelief. Not that she thought Liz was being dishonest, but the very thought of spending time with Eliza outside the office thrilled her to her very fingertips. Wow! What a privilege. That was reason enough for Celia to persevere.

To address Celia's sexual addiction presented a greater challenge. Liz understood the addictions as spiritual problems. She needed to communicate it in such a way that Celia also made that connection. She decided that the greatest gift she could give Celia was a specifically designed program.

"Celia, there is an excellent resource nearby that I highly recommend. It's the Living Waters Program.[8] It's an in-depth healing, teaching and discipleship series. Their goal is to lay a foundation for sexual and relational wholeness. Here is their brochure."

"Thank you, Eliza. I'll call them when I get home. This brochure says I have to send for an application, but it doesn't say when the thirty weeks begin or how much it costs."

"It was probably designed as a 'litmus test' to see if applicants are serious about recovery. I believe this is God's answer to your prayers for sexual purity."

Celia did not hestitate. As soon as she got home she called Living Waters. Their next class would start in six weeks. She marveled at God's timing and financial provision. Within a matter of three weeks, Celia had filled out the application, completed her interview and paid the first half of the tuition.

Her expectations soared. She just knew she had masturbated for the very last time in her life. Celia was confident that her shame and guilt was finally behind her. She had already begun to wonder how many times she could confess comforting herself and God would be willing to forgive her and believe her promise to never do it again.

She hated violating her body with foreign objects. She remembered her torrent of tears after practicing that behavior which spurned her resolve to quit. Finally, God had demonstrated that he heard her prayers and answered far beyond her wildest dreams.

The reality of a forty-five year old addiction came crashing in on Celia two weeks into the program. Bam! It happened again. She was devastated. Wasn't Living Waters God's answer to her addiction? Was God playing a game with her? Had she wasted her money on a program that wasn't going to work? So many questions bombarded Celia's thoughts. She cried out to God.

Her sobbing slowly subsided, her words gradually gave way to complete silence. Exhausted, she remained on her knees. In a moment a parade of past experiences marched across her recollection. God was speaking.

"You have masturbated as many as five or six times in one day. You don't do that any more. You have comforted yourself at least once a day. You don't do that any more. You have prayed for forgiveness on a weekly basis, but you don't have to do that anymore. This is the first time in more than a month; I'm so proud of you. Be patient with yourself. I have heard your prayer. Living Waters is my answer for you."

The tears began to flow once again. This time they were tears of joy. Celia knew one day she wouldn't even remember the last time she practiced "the secret" she learned so many years ago.

The road to victory twisted and turned around frustrations and setbacks. It traveled uphill and downhill as Celia struggled to put into place the messages of encouragement and hope she received from the Lord and from Liz.

Sending E-mail messages provided an added incentive for coach and athlete to communicate. Sessions decreased from three times a week to twice a week to once a week to bi-monthly and eventually monthly. Celia's commitment to therapy paid a dividend of increasing maturity. However, there were times when old patterns of destructive thinking and behaving crept into her days.

From: Celia C. Canterbury
To: Eliza
Subject: Hurting!

Eliza,

I know you keep telling me the same thing over and over again. I don't know why I can't seem to get the message straight. I am lost somewhere down the corridors of gluttony. I am supposed to go to my nutritionist on Friday, but I don't think there is a reason for going.

I have not been faithful to the program for the past three weeks, and each day I purpose and pray to be victorious, but invaribly I will eat maybe just one little something that spoils my resolve. Then I find myself riding that same roller coaster. I am going to bed and cry myself to sleep.

                   Celia

From: Eliza
To: Celia C. Canterbury
Subject: Re: Hurting!

Celia,

In Jesus' name, stop this!! This is not from the Lord!! It is time for you to stand up and allow the Lord to win this through and with you. It is a matter of being diligent to the discipline he has set before you and not being the perfectionist who throws up her hands and goes "hog wild" when she makes one mistake.

I want you to go to the nutritionist and be accountable. That is something that I feel is necessary for you. This week is Easter week...are you speaking death or life into what the Lord has done in you?

Celia, in Jesus' name, stop this line of thinking of self-pity and self-incrimi-

nation!! Enough!! It is long past time for you to go up to the mountain and be willing to offer all this up so God alone can provide the ram in the thicket!! Don't lie down and cry!! There is a battle raging!!
Love, Eliza
P. S. Yes, this means YOU!!!

    Celia valued Liz's words whether they were face to face, talking on the phone or corresponding by E-mail. She determined to be obedient to what Liz advised her to do. She knew working with Liz was an exceptional gift from God. So she provided a platform from which Liz received assistance for continued therapy by E-mailing her before each session.

From: Celia C. Canterbury
To: Eliza
Subject: Tenderly Apologetic and Thankful

My dearest Eliza,
I am so tenderly apologetic for the series of questions that were necessary because I neglected to E-mail you. I know how much you love and care for me. I should have been more thoughtful. In the future I will make sure I E-mail you ahead of time.

Thank you so much for our sessions. I appreciate how much you have poured yourself into my recovery. Thank you for your prayers and cards and phone calls, for saying the hard things and being an obedient vessel. Thank you for modeling God's love.

Because of you, I am beginning to see the light at the end of the tunnel. Celia C. Canterbury a whole, mature, vibrant woman facing life's challenges totally depending on my Heavenly Papa. I love you so much, Eliza.

Forever grateful,
Celia

CHAPTER 7 ❧ SITTING BY THE BROOK WITH JESUS

Bam! Bam! Bam! Celia knelt beside the seven foot cross and began to pound her nail as hard as she could. Living Waters had finally answered her unasked question. Where was Jesus when E. F. molested her day after day, week after week, year after year for over a decade until he died?

Celia pounded the nail again and again and sobbed, "Jesus was on the cross dying for his sin and for mine; now I can forgive my dad and myself." She struck the nail several more times. She now had a reason not to hate Janna Cherie; "I forgive you, Mom, whether you knew or not." Her hand went up as the tears streamed down; "I pound this nail for forgiveness for my sexual addiction, Lord -- for all the times I promised it would never happen again and it did."

Smack! She pounded it for her food addiction -- the sin of gluttony. As an adult she recognized her responsibility for the decisions she made regarding her generational pain.

"In your name, Jesus, I nail everything to the cross and receive your forgiveness. I know now your heart was breaking every time I was raped by my dad. You suffered with me every time I was abused by my mom and violated by others. I confess every little twinge and every humongous gouge of pain."

Celia pounded that nail until she released all the guilt and shame of her childhood abuse and her sinful behaviors because of it. There was something cleansing about kneeling at the cross and nailing all her pain and agony there. It was the ultimate symbol of taking her sinful self, her hatred for Janna Cherie, her inability to mourn and forgive her dad and releasing it all in the capable loving arms of a forgiving heavenly Father.

For the first time Celia *knew* without a doubt that Jesus loved her. Oh, Liz kept telling her in as many ways as she knew how. Until that night of full release, Celia had only accepted it by faith hoping with all her heart that Liz's reassurance would become a reality. Although the new birth had happened over forty years ago, Celia now fully embraced it, "Therefore, if anyone is in Christ, he is a new creation; the old has gone, the new has come!"[1]

Ring, ring, ring. Who would be calling her at this hour of the night? "Hello."

"Hello, this is the Emergency Medical Team near Portland, Oregon. We have your husband here, Nathan Canterbury, and we believe he has had a heart attack. We should be at the hospital in about thirty minutes. You can call about that time, and the nurse on duty will give you more specific details."

"Why didn't they just wait until they got to the hospital to call me?" Celia mused.

She began to pray for Nathan and for the next thirty minutes to pass quickly. Nathan did not leave her when she was fragmented into sixteen selves. He endured rejection from personalities who refused to share a bed with him and criticized his decision-making process. Nathan was never ashamed to walk with Celia in public even when she carried Snuggles and Pooh and sucked her thumb for everyone in the community to see.

Celia tried not to panic. "Lord, please don't take Nathan. He's such a wonderful husband. I wouldn't have recovered without his support. Lord, please let him be all right. Amen."

"Hello, Portland Community Hospital Emergency."

"Hello, I'm Celia Canterbury; I understand my husband, Nathan, was transported there."

"The ambulance just arrived. It has been confirmed that he did have a heart attack. This is a teaching hospital, and we have an excellent Cardiac Care Unit. Our chief cardiologist is on staff tonight. He is rushing Nathan into surgery as we speak. Call back tomorrow around 10:00 A. M., and the doctor will be available to talk with you."

"Thank you, Jesus, for taking care of Nathan. Please see him through the surgery. Give me wisdom to know what to do. Portland is three thousand miles away, but I want to be with him. Would you please make it possible for me to go?"

Celia sat down at the organ and began to play softly, "When peace like a river attendeth my way, when sorrows like sea billows roll, whatever my lot, thou hast taught me to say, It is well, it is well with my soul."[1] Liz had sung that song in her ear on more than one occasion. Now was the perfect time to once again find comfort in that special hymn.

Much to her surprise, she had taken Jesus up on his offer and sat down beside him under the large Oak tree on the banks of the rippling brook. Serenity enveloped her. Celia crawled under her covers and went fast asleep.

"Hello Celia, this is Stewart, Nathan's supervisor. I called to let you know that the company will pay for your airfare to Portland. Stay as long as it takes to bring him home. Send us the receipts for your plane tickets, hotel accommodations, car rental and restaurant bills. We will reimburse you. We are praying for you and Nathan. Keep us posted on how he is getting along. If you need anything, don't hesitate to call. Nathan is an asset to our company; we will do whatever we can to help."

"Wow. This business of sitting by the brook with Jesus sure pays exceptional dividends," thought Celia.

"Hello Mrs. Canterbury, I'm Dr. Corday. Your husband is going to be just fine. He had a ninety-eight percent blockage in one artery. I put a stent in it last night. He has a ninety-five percent blockage in another artery. We will have to wait several days before I can put in the other stent. You were lucky. If Mr. Canterbury had gotten here five minutes later, he would not have survived."

"Dr. Corday, thank you for taking care of my husband, but that wasn't luck. The Lord answered my prayer not to let Nathan die. I'll be in town tonight. I am looking forward to meeting you."

Nathan's hospital stay lasted only a week, but his period of convalescence continued for four long months. His medical coverage did not include short term disability benefits. Celia and Nathan had to make major financial decisions.

They reviewed their financial commitments. God provided all their needs, yet he challenged Celia to trust him with her ministry to hurting families. Then stark reality slapped her squarely in the face. Celia had to layoff all her employees and shut down the ministry. No matter how she tried there wasn't any other conclusion.

Celia became angry with God. Wasn't she being obedient to his calling upon her life as a Minister? Wasn't she providing a source of income for the precious ones God had entrusted to her care as their Executive Director? Weren't they providing the community a much needed service as well as helping their clients strengthen their relationships with the Lord Jesus? How could this be happening? Certainly, God must be mistaken.

Her period of mourning ignited conflict in their marriage. Nathan couldn't do anything right.

"Can't you see I'm hurting? I need you to comfort me. Why are you standing there as though you don't know what to do? You see me crying. Why don't you hand me a tissue and just hold me?"

Even if Nathan wanted to comfort Celia, her icy, piercing accusations made him feel like recoiling...but he didn't. He lovingly wrapped his arms around her and let her cry. Celia sobbed as though her heart would nearly break.

Her period of mourning was interrupted with an unusual message. There was no audible sound. It was an indelible thought and a stirring in her spirit. *Since Nathan has had a heart attack, it would be prudent to relocate closer to your daughters.* Celia didn't say anything, but contemplated the idea.

Days passed. Weeks passed. There was still a restlessness that indicated she needed to approach the subject with Nathan. The very evening Celia determined to discuss the possibility of moving, her neighbor stopped by that afternoon in a frenzy.

She asked if Celia had heard the latest news. It appeared the city planned to develop the land across the street. This necessitated buying their houses to develop a park so that it abated the towpath the city put in two years earlier.

Her neighbor ranted frantically about not having the money to move. She didn't know what to do. She was adamant she had it on good authority it was unmistakably going to happen.

Celia asked, "How do you know this isn't a rumor?"

Apparently during a city council meeting, one of the councilmen let it slip. He wasn't suppose to divulge that part of the city's plan. Several concerned citizens asked questions, but they received only political answers. By the atmosphere in the meeting, it was obvious that plans to redevelop the east side of the street were a great possibility.

Since Celia knew the City Planning Commissioner personally, she called to verify her neighbor's information. Sure enough, without divulging any confidential plans, he confirmed the city's intentions at some future date.

Incredible described the Lord's timing. Nathan and Celia agreed to employ a strategy to move forward. There was no doubt about it--this next step definitely necessitated sitting by the brook with Jesus. Relocating presented a major change in their lives as they were also moving into their senior years.

As Celia and Jesus sat under the shady oak he began to speak into her thoughts his strategy for their immediate future. They first had to settle all of their financial responsibilities and live debt-free. "Woefully inadequate" best described her disability check. She and Nathan decided Celia had to acquire some form of additional income.

They prayed at each juncture of the many new challenges. Celia moved into their apartment first leaving Nathan in the house until it sold. The two critical decisions were: 1) finding a fundamental evangelical church with which to fellowship and 2) selecting a location that considered Nathan's travel time to work and the proximity to their daughters' homes. The idea of being near their daughters, son-in-laws and grandchildren stepped up the process.

The days turned into weeks and the weeks became months as her heart struggled to find a new spiritual home.

"Lord, would you please direct me to a local church that is African American and in the denomination where I was ordained?" Celia pleaded.

She had visited so many congregations, but the result was the same. Celia walked away empty. She needed a place where she could grow spiritually. She felt she had lost fifty years of her life never actually living up to her potential because of her multiple personalities. She desperately needed a church family that would embrace her with all her idiosyncracies.

It was a sunny afternoon in early December when Celia found herself driving down the main thoroughfare. She drove past a church in her denomination.

"Turn around and pull into that church's parking lot," an inescapable thought interrupted her.

"Lord, I *know* this is a white church," Celia protested.

"This is where I want you to worship on Sunday," their dialogue continued.

"Lord Jesus, I asked you for an African American church in my denomination. I really was counting on you answering one hundred percent of my prayer. Fifty-percent does not make me happy."

The remainder of the week passed without incident. That was quite all right with Celia. She had experienced enough drama in the past ten years to last her a lifetime. Sunday morning dawned with an unexpected brilliance of both sunshine and 'son'shine.

Celia stepped into the narthex decked out in a burgundy suit with shoes and a purse to match. She wore a velvet hat with a four inch brim that sloped to the right side adorned with cubic zirconia and rhinestones that sparkled in the sunlight.

Warmth and friendliness permeated the air. She was greeted and escorted to a Sunday school class. The teacher and students embraced Celia like a long lost friend. They introduced themselves and expressed delight in having her visit their class without a hint of insincerity. She received a Sunday school book, and they didn't ask for it back either. That impressed Celia. She felt valued. Not only that, she shared her prayer request to sell her house, to find a new residence and to be obedient to God's direction in her life. The teacher prayed for all the prayer requests and called Celia and Nathan by name.

Wow! Even though Celia's acceptance in Sunday school was amazing, it paled in comparison to morning worship service. The Worship Pastor was vibrant and excited about his faith--so much so that he invited the congregation to stand and enter into worship as though Jesus Christ were coming within the hour and that this would be their last opportunity to praise him on this side of heaven.

"Go Tell it on the Mountain" opened their celebration. Celia really felt at ease because it is a well-known Negro Spiritual. To her delight she basked in "Infant Holy, Infant Lowly" played by the Handbell Choir. "Silent Night" ushered her into the very serenity of the Christmas season. When she thought praise and worship had reached it pinnacle, the Worship Pastor sang "Welcome to Our World." His voice was rich with clarity, volume and purity.

Then the crowning moment finally arrived. The Senior Pastor took his text from Isaiah 9:6-7. His sermon title was "Mighty God." Celia began to write in her bulletin the basics of his message: Jesus has the power to save you. Jesus has the power to support you. Jesus has the power to strengthen you. God can only guard and protect what you give to him.

The tears streamed down Celia's face. For the first time she fully understood Psalm 42:1, "As the deer pants for streams of water, so my soul pants for you, O God."[1] There she sat lapping up every word that eloquently flowed from the pastor's lips. She looked no further. God had answered her prayer far beyond her wildest expectations.

No one knew her story. No one knew she had left everyone behind, even Nathan, in search for a new beginning. No one knew Celia's desperate need to be accepted, loved and appreciated. Only God knew what Celia longed for most -- a home for her heart among the children of God.

She fought the cold, the wind and the snow and pressed her way to midweek prayer and Bible study. The intimacy of this smaller group was utterly contagious. Celia sat beside the pastor's wife. She embraced her gentle sweet spirit -- the perfect qualities for a church's First Lady. Secretly, Celia purposed to win her way into her heart as a special friend.

Celia's exhuberant worship style rocked the church as she introduced them to her African American way of spiritual interaction. A hearty "Amen, Praise the Lord or Hallelujah" permeated the otherwise silent worship. Celia talked back to the Pastor when he preached, and he talked back to her. It was usually impossible for her to respond in any other way. Not only was it her heritage, but the Lord Jesus went to "hell" and back to give Celia the life he created her to have.

Being vocal wasn't always her forte'. There were so many times all Celia could do was wipe her tears as she remembered being fragmented into so many selves, she didn't even know her name. Being vocal wasn't all ways her forte' because there were so many times all she could do was sway back and forth, nod her head with consent and sing in a whisper, '*Change my heart, oh God. Make it ever true. Change my heart, oh God. May I be like you. You are the potter; I am the clay.*

Mold me and make me; this is what I pray. Change my heart, oh God. Make it ever true. Change my heart, oh God. May I be like you.'

Bubbly and vivacious Celia lit up the church with her smile and her parade of endless stylish hats. She was unaware that her presence and warmth so affected the congregation, that the Senior Pastor asked Celia to preach.

Through the prompting of God's Holy Spirit, Celia gave her testimony of sexual abuse. Celia's sermon, from Joel chapter two, focused on the first part of verse twenty-five, "The LORD says, I will give you back what you lost to the stripping locusts, the cutting locusts, the swarming locusts, and the hopping locusts..."

She recognized her locusts as the invading army of incest -- being raped for twelve years. The stripping locusts snatched her innocence at three years old. The cutting locusts cut off her ability to live a normal life as a whole person. The swarming locusts tested her desire of ever being free of the craziness in her life. The hopping locusts discouraged her belief that she would ever be forgiven because she had done to others what she learned from her dad.

The Lord restored everything the locusts had taken in an exceedingly abundant way. He gave her a cherished husband, Nathan, and a new city, then a new Pastor and First Lady whom she loved dearly. God blessed her with a new church family, a Sunday school class, and special friends. He gave her a new ministry encouraging others through life's struggles. Celia's testimony of God's faithfulness after fifty-six years encouraged the congregation to hold on to God's personal promises.

Amazingly she is on the brink of a new adventure of building a new house. She and Nathan scouted the area and found the perfect three-acre corner lot. Celia could hardly believe it. All of God's provisions were far more than she had ever hoped. The message reminded Celia of God's matchless love.

After worship, there were some who confided their brokenness because of incest and other forms of abuse. Celia prayed with them, cried with others and embraced them all. She understood one of the reasons why the Lord wanted her to tell her story.

Their warm reception encouraged Celia. So, early in the morning she found herself drawn to that rippling brook where Jesus waited for her. They talked with each other about what concerned them the most. Occasionally, Celia was admonished because the Lord knew she could do better and not be drawn into old destructive patterns. There were other moments when she sang the Lord a lullaby, *'Knowing you, Jesus, knowing you. There is no greater thing. You're my all, you're my best, you're my joy my righteousness, and I love you, Lord.'*

More than ever before Celia could see that she is on a journey. The loud is becoming serene; awkwardness and immaturity are giving way to poise and confidence. Self-centeredness has been catapulted into a greater display of the mind of Christ -- putting others first.

Sitting by the brook with Jesus has become Celia's lifestyle. She begins each day spending time in prayer, reading her Bible, playing the piano or organ and singing love songs to her heavenly Papa. When perplexing challenges presents themselves, she runs to Jesus no matter what she is doing at the time -- shopping, housework or driving.

Sometimes she still finds herself at the brink of worrying, but Celia prays about what's troubling her and goes back to sleep instantly. She never thought a peaceful sleep was possible; neither did she believe Liz when she said, "I see a bright future ahead of you." Now, she enjoys both realities.

Sitting by the brook with Jesus allows Celia to treasure precious moments with her mother, Janna Cherie. She finds herself enjoying their visits and praying together. Celia covets the wisdom in her words. Her angry, abusive mother has mellowed over the years. God taught Janna Cherie how to love and has given her the ability to express it openly.

The morning air was crisp and the bright sunlight beckoned Janna Cherie. Being in her late 80's was no deterrent. She invited Celia to go with her to an annual rib-burn-off in early July. To her surprise Janna

Cherie had made preparations for them to ride the city bus. Celia hadn't ridden a bus since she was a teenager. Their time together allowed her to mend broken dreams of having a mother who was capable of both showing and expressing love.

They laughed together as they visited the different booths trying to decide which ribs to buy. Being downtown brought back happy childhood memories that had been overshadowed by abuse. They stopped by the Peanut Shoppe to reminense. Janna Cherie bought sherbert while Celia just had to have their delicious cashews.

The hours passed quickly, and it was time to catch the bus. Celia and Janna Cherie made special memories that day. Never had they ridden the city bus together. This was also their first time enjoying the festivities of the rib-burn-off.

Celia remembered threatening to discontinue her sessions with Liz when she approached the subject of Janna Cherie. She felt it was impossible to relate to her mother in any other way than what she had known all her life. Thankfully, Liz finally taught Celia how to be an adult with her mom. Now, she and Janna Cherie had established a loving relationship that would last the rest of their lives.

Celia recognized that living in the past was robbing her of a future of joy, peace and happiness. Having a new life, a new way of living with Jesus Christ was enough demonstration of God's love for Celia. To live each day without being negatively affected by the pain in her past was more than she ever dreamed was possible.

Liz had given her numerous tools with which to face unexpected challenges. Celia began to integrate them into her daily life. Some struggles presented disappointments and tears; nevertheless, Celia faced the pain realizing that happier days would finally come. Constantly she revisited her archives of resources. Liz was thorough in providing information Celia could use long after their working together ended. Perplexed with self-destructive thoughts she looked for the 'Thought Record' Liz had given her.

Celia wrote the date. She then completed the five-step procedure that included: 1) the situation, 2) her feelings, 3) automatic thoughts,

4) realistic answers, and 5) the outcome. She took great pleasure in not needing to confront that exercise very often even though she found it to be quite helpful.

The time had come to reestablish broken relationships in her family. She determined to follow the example Liz had established. She began to complete "Relationship Graphs"[2] for each family member. The process of writing down all the positive and negative experiences they shared, asking for forgiveness, making amends and expressing appreciation for the good times commenced the necessary healing. Family ties meant a great deal to Celia. So she remained diligent in her endeavor to rectify her past.

When she became petrified after her fender bender, she called Pete, but much to her surprise their Relationship Graph indicated they had not spent much time together over the years. Her immediate goal swung into action. She began to call Pete and ask his advice about professional matters. He was a genius with computers, web design and hosting. It was great spending precious moments with him.

Two months after Celia began to mend her relationship with Pete, he announced his doctor discovered an advanced stage-four cancerous growth. Once a growth moves to the final stage it is dubious whether chemotherapy would be advantageous; however, Pete and his doctor were optimistic.

Sickness has a way of bringing families together. Gratefully this became true for the Abernathy's. Justina, a Registered Nurse, began to do what she does brilliantly. She accompanied Pete each week for his chemotherapy and began to take him when he was incapable of driving. Celia gladly filled that role when Justina was hospitalized and released to convalescence for the following months.

Six weeks walked across the corridors of time. Pete and Celia bonded for the first time in their lives. He gave her advice to handle some pressing matters. They laughed together and made new memories. Pete loved the Lord and said on numerous occasions that his cup was running over.

When participating in corporate worship became impossible, Celia called the family together and planned worship services in Pete's home. They sang hymns, read the Scriptures, enjoyed a robust testimonial period, served communion and listened to a sermon. Pete was excited about the experience and declared his testimony of God's faithfulness. He told his family that God had blessed him with excellent health for fifty-nine years, twenty days, thirteen hours, ten minutes and twenty seconds for which he was truly grateful.

Celia listened intently to Pete's advice as they spent precious hours and days together. He had suffered no side effects from the chemo and almost no pain. After nine months, Pete breathed his last, leaving Celia with no regrets.

Pete's death further inspired Celia. More than anything her constant prayer became more fervent to totally devote herself to being all that she had the potential of becoming. Whether it was cooking, washing dishes, washing the clothes or merely driving along the highway, she found herself humming, *'Lord, prepare me to be a sanctuary, pure and holy, tried and true; With thanksgiving, I'll be a living sanctuary for you.'*

Life continued to present its challenges. Celia still experienced body memories that startled her on occasions when Nathan failed to make his presence known. Yet, each day was manageable. Much to her surprise and delight she could actually live independently of Liz. There were times when she and Nathan needed professional guidance so they talked with Ray.

Celia and Nathan have begun to explore some sexual retraining assignments from a chapter in Restoring the Pleasure.[3] They discovered that their beliefs about sexual pleasure are similar, but Celia still feels uncomfortable at times expressing intimacy.

Although Liz had given Celia some excellent resources for her arsenal of life skills, she and Nathan periodically still need Ray's expertise so further healing could take place. He recommended The Gift of Sex,[4] which they are finding quite enlightening. However, this delicate matter causes Celia to shy away sometimes. So she knows it's time to take a trip to the rippling brook so Jesus can encourage her and give her his grace to face her recollections and fears. After talking with the Lord for a while as the cool breeze whistles through her hair, Jesus asked Celia to revisit an E-mail Liz had sent her.

Dear Celia,

We are always soldiers in God's army. Right? If so, a soldier practices and works at various disciplines at all times, even when you are not in war because he never knows when a battle will come. A soldier needs to always be diligent and ready.

Remember God asked Abraham to offer Isaac as a sacrifice. I think it sort of boils down to the reality that being able to do what you want to do when you want to do it and as much as you want to do it is something that has been pretty important to you due to the lack of freedom through much of your life.

That may well be the Isaac he is asking for now -- not just the public face of it, but the true motives and spirit of that precious held value.

Blessed Easter to you!!

Love,
Eliza

Oh, Celia cringed as she read the E-mail. What Jesus was asking her to do was to be disciplined.

"Okay, Lord. I surrender my recollections and fears to you. I will be disciplined in every area of my life. No more doing what I want to do when I want to do it and as much as I want."

Immediately, Celia obediently entered into a 'Daniel Fast'[5] for forty days. Without even trying, she began to lose weight. Some of her clothes soon became too large. She established an exercise regiment on her treadmill. She was well on her way to overcoming her food addiction.

Today, Celia finds new strength and faces challenges that reassure her that a new era has dawned. She realizes that she misses Nathan and asks him to consider working only five days a week since his job keeps him constantly traveling. Without hesitating, Nathan obliges his wife because he enjoys pleasing her. His being home on a more regular basis is allowing Celia to slowly overcome her fears. Nathan, too, recognizes Celia's growing trust in his love and protection. He sees that she is more relaxed with his expressions of affection.

So, with a twinkle in his eye, Nathan walked to the top of the stairs -- minus a step or two. Celia forged her way down the steps -- minus a stair or two. Their bodies met and spoke a language they both understood.

Nathan gingerly coaxed his wife with tender kisses and an irresistible embrace. The night was young as was their playfulness. As purposeful as a craftsman he wooed Celia to a point of ecstasy. Her laughter permeated the room.

It was both a victory and a delight that Celia found comfort in Nathan's embrace, body to body, breath to breath, uninhibited, lively with giggles and enveloped with thanksgiving. A godly husband's unconditional love finally ushered in the dawning of an ebony princess.

𝔉AMILIES OF 𝔙ICTORY 𝔐INISTRIES, 𝔍NC.

ℭARES 𝔄BOUT 𝔜OU!

𝔓LEASE 𝔖END 𝔘S 𝔜OUR 𝔓RAYER 𝔑EQUESTS.

You may contact us at:

P. O. BOX 3075
LEXINGTON, OH 44904

1 - 877 - 285 - 1175   PIN: 2889

www.fovm.ws
celia@fovm.ws

NOTES

Chapter One

1. Raymond Bial, (1999). <u>One-Room School,</u> (p. 10), Boston: Houghton Mifflin Company.
2. Virginia E. McCormick, (2001). <u>Educational Architecture in Ohio: From One-Room School and Carnegie Libraries to Community Education Villages</u>, (p. 80), Kent, OH: The Kent State University Press.

Chapter Five

1. <u>The Picture Bible</u>, (1978). Elgin, IL: David C. Cook Publishing Co.
2. Edward F. Murphy, (1992). <u>The Handbook for Spiritual Warfare</u>, Nashville, TN: Thomas Nelson Publishers.
3. James G. Friesen, (1991). <u>Uncovering the Mystery of MPD: Its Shocking Origins...Its Surprising Cure</u>, Nashville, TN: Thomas Nelson Publishers.
4. Ibid. p. 222

Chapter Six

1. Liz, (1998). M.S., LPCC, Marriage & Family Therapist.
2. Sandra D. Wilson, (1990). <u>Released from Shame: Recovery for Adult Children of Dysfunctional Families</u>, Downers Grove, IL: InterVarsity Press.
3. Ibid., p. 167
4. Ibid., p. 169
5. Pat Springle, (1994). <u>Trusting: Learning Who and How to Trust Again</u>, Ann Arbor, MI: Servant Publications.
6. Ibid., p. 190
7. Ibid., p. 195
8. Andrew Comiskey, (2000). <u>Living Waters: Pursuing Sexual & Relational Wholeness in Christ</u>, Anaheim, CA: Desert Stream Press.

Chapter Seven

1. The Holy Bible: New International Version. (1996). (p. 478), Grand Rapids, MI: Zondervan Bible Publishers.
2. John W. James, & Russell Friedman, (1998). The Grief Recovery Handbook: The Action Program For Moving Beyond Death, Divorce, And Other Losses (Rev. ed.), (p. 115), New York: HarperPerennial Publishers, Inc.
3. Clifford Penner & Joyce Penner, (1993). Restoring the Pleasure, (p. 168), Nashville, TN: Thomas Nelson Publishers.
4. Clifford Penner & Joyce Penner, (2003). The Gift of Sex: A Guide to Sexual Fulfillment, Nashville, TN: W Publishing Group.
5. The Holy Bible: New International Version, (1996). (p. 747), Grand Rapids, MI: Zondervan Bible Publishers.

BIBLIOGRAPHY

Bial, R. (1999). One-Room School. Boston: Houghton Mifflin Company.

Comiskey, A. (2000). Living Waters: Pursuing Sexual & Relational Wholeness in Christ. Anaheim, CA: Desert Stream Press.

Friesen, J. G. (1991). Uncovering the Mystery of MPD: Its Shocking Origins...Its Surprising Cure. Nashville, TN: Thomas Nelson Publishers.

Friesen, J. G. (1992) More Than Survivors: Conversations With Multiple-Personality Clients. San Bernardino, CA: Here's Life Publishers, Inc.

Graves, B. E. (1993). School Ways: The Planning and Design of American Schools. New York: McGraw-Hill, Inc.

James, J. W. & Friedman, R. (1998). The Grief Recovery Handbook: The Action Program For Moving Beyond Death, Divorce, And Other Losses (Rev. ed.). New York: HarperPerennial Publishers, Inc.

McCormick, V. E. (2001). Educational Architecture in Ohio: From One-Room School and Carnegie Libraries to Community Education Villages. Kent, OH: The Kent State University Press.

Murphy, E. F. (1992). The Handbook for Spiritual Warfare. Nashville, TN: Thomas Nelson Publishers.

Penner, C. & Penner, J. (1993). Restoring the Pleasure. Nashville, TN: Thomas Nelson Publishers.

Penner, C. & Penner, J. (2003). <u>The Gift of Sex: A Guide to Sexual Fulfillment</u>. Nashville, TN: W Publishing Group.

Springle, P. (1994). <u>Trusting: Learning Who and How to Trust Again</u>. Ann Arbor, MI: Servant Publications.

<u>The Holy Bible: New International Version</u>. (1996). Grand Rapids, MI: Zondervan Bible Publishers.

<u>The Picture Bible</u>. (1978). Elgin, IL: David C. Cook Publishing Co.

Wilson, S. D. (1990). <u>Released from Shame: Recovery for Adult Children of Dysfunctional Families</u>. Downers Grove, IL: InterVarsity Press.